DONATED BY

Dr. & Mrs. A. J. F. O'Reilly

AND

H. J. Heinz Company

The
Holy
Surprise
of Right Now

WITHDRAWN
FROM THE COLLECTION
CARNEGIE LIBRARY OF PITTSBURGH

CLP-East Liberty	

PS
3515
.A9877
H6
1996

CARNEGIE
LIBRARY OF
PITTSBURGH

East Liberty Branch Library

DEMCO

Other Books by Samuel Hazo

POETRY

The Past Won't Stay Behind You
Silence Spoken Here
Nightwords
The Color of Reluctance
Thank a Bored Angel
To Paris
Quartered

Once for the Last Bandit
Twelve Poems
Blood Rights
My Sons in God
Listen with the Eye
The Quiet Wars
Discovery

FICTION

Stills
The Wanton Summer Air
The Very Fall of the Sun
Inscripts

TRANSLATIONS

The Pages of Day and Night
(Poems of Adonis)

Lebanon: Twenty Poems for One Love
(Poems of Nadia Tueni)

Transformations of the Lover

The Growl of Deeper Waters
(Essays of Denis de Rougemont)

The Blood of Adonis

CRITICISM

Smithereened Apart:
A Critique of Hart Crane

ESSAYS

The Pittsburgh That Stays Within You
The Feast of Icarus
The Rest Is Prose

PLAYS

Solos
Until I'm Not Here Anymore

MY 16 '98

The Holy Surprise of Right Now

Selected & New Poems

Samuel Hazo

PS
3515
.A9877
H6
1996

THE UNIVERSITY OF ARKANSAS PRESS

Fayetteville

1996

CARNEGIE LIBRARY OF PITTSBURGH
EAST LIBERTY BRANCH
5920 RALPH MUNN MALL
PITTSBURGH, PA 15206

CARNEGIE LIBRARY OF PITTSBURGH

Copyright 1959, 1962, 1965, 1968, 1972, 1981, 1983, 1988,
1993, 1996 by Samuel Hazo

All rights reserved
Manufactured in the United States of America

oo   99   98   97   96   5   4   3   2   1

Designed by Gail Carter

♾ The paper used in this publication meets the minimum
requirements of the American National Standard for Permanence
of Paper for Printed Library Materials Z39.48-1984.

Library of Congress Cataloging-in-Publication Data
Hazo, Samuel John.
The holy surprise of right now :
selected and new poems / Samuel Hazo.
p.   cm.
Includes index.
ISBN 1-55728-427-X (cloth : alk. paper). —
ISBN 1-55728-428-8 (pbk. : alk. paper)
I. Title.
PS3515.A9877H6   1996   95-52047
811'.54—dc20   CIP

For Mary Anne
and
Sam & Dawn
and
Robert
and
in memory of Kak

Acknowledgments

Grateful acknowledgment is made to the editors and publishers of the following magazines or books in which some of the poems in this volume originally appeared:

*American Scholar, Antaeus, Antioch Review,
Beloit Poetry Journal, Boulevard,
Borestone Mountain Awards, Carolina Quarterly,
Cedar Rock, Chicago Choice, Commonweal, Critic,
Crosscurrents, Four Quarters, Georgia Review,
Greenfield Review, Harper's, Hollins Critic,
Hudson Review, Image, Kansas City Review,
Kenyon Review, Malahat Review, Mediterranean Review,
Michigan Quarterly Review, Minnesota Review,
Mississippi Review, New Directions in Prose and Poetry 41,
New Letters, New Orleans Review, New World Writing,
New York Times, Ontario Review, Organica, Painted Bird,
Pittsburgh Post-Gazette, Poetry Miscellany,
Prairie Schooner, Sagatrieb, Saturday Review,
Sewanee Review, Southern Review, Tar River Poetry,
Texas Observer, Texas Quarterly, Transatlantic Review,
Virginia Quarterly Review,* and *Yale Review.*

With the exception of the final twenty-six selections, poems in this book have been drawn from *Discovery* (1959) and *The Quiet Wars* (1962), published by Sheed and Ward; *My Sons in God* (1965), *Blood Rights* (1968), and *Once for the Last Bandit* (1972), published by the University of Pittsburgh Press; *To Paris* (1981) and *Thank a Bored Angel* (1983), published by New Directions; *Silence Spoken Here* (1988), published by Marlboro Press; and *The Past Won't Stay Behind You* (1993), published by the University of Arkansas Press.

The first section of "At the Site of the Memorial" is engraved at the entrance to the park in Harrisburg honoring Pennsylvanians awarded the Congressional Medal of Honor from the Civil War to the present.

Contents

The
Holy
Surprise
of Right Now

POSTSCRIPT TO MANY LETTERS

For Robert George Hazo

While other brothers meet and talk like foes
or strangers or alumni—hostile, cool,
or banal—brotherhood is still our binding.
Somehow we have survived disintegration
since the quiet Pittsburgh afternoons we walked
in rain bareheaded, scarfless, flaunting health,
the nights we smoked large academic pipes
and read and talked philosophy, the years
of seminars and uniforms and trips
and letters postmarked Paris, Quantico,
Beirut, Jerusalem, and San Francisco.

Nothing has changed or failed and still we have
"the same heroes and think the same men fools."
Our heroes still are individuals
resolved to face their private absolutes.
We see the fool in all who fail themselves
by choice and turn all promise cold with talk.
A Levantine who saw such folly done
two thousand years ago grew bored with life
and said only the unborn were worth blessing.
Not sticks, not any, not the sharpest stones
can bruise or break the unbegotten bones.

Yet, fools and our few heroes will persist.
We cannot bless the unborn flesh or wish
our times and cities back to countrysides
when wigwams coned into a twist of poles.
The future holds less answers than the past.
Salvation lies in choice, in attitude,
in faith that mocks glib gospelers who leave
the name of Jesus whitewashed on a cliff.
We still can shun what shames or shams
the day and keep as one our vigor in the bond
of blood where love is fierce but always fond.

3

TO MY MOTHER

Had you survived that August afternoon
of Bright's Disease, you would be sixty-three,
and I would not be rummaging for words
to plot or rhyme what I would speak to you.

Tonight I found a diary you kept
in nineteen twenty-eight, and while I read
your script in English, Arabic, and Greek,
I grudged those perished years and nearly wept

and cursed whatever god I often curse
because I scarcely knew one day with you
or heard you sing or call me by my name.
I know you were a teacher and a nurse

and sang at all the summer festivals.
You made one scratched recording of a song
I often play when no one else is home,
but that is all I have to keep you real.

The rest exists in fragile photographs,
a sudden memoir in my father's eyes
and all the anecdotes of thirty years
remembered like a portrait torn in half

and torn in half again until a word
deciphered in a diary rejoins
these tatters in my mind to form your face
as magically as music overheard

can summon and assemble everything
about a day we thought forever past.
For one recovered second you are near.
I almost hear you call to me and sing

before the world recoils and returns . . .
I have no monument, my beautiful,
to offer you except these patterned lines.
They cannot sound the silences that burn

and burn, although I try to say at last
there lives beyond this treachery of words
your life in me anew and in that peace
where nothing is to come and nothing past.

PREFACE TO A POETRY READING

Since eyes are deaf and ears are blind to words
in all their ways, I speak the sounds I write,
hoping you see what somehow stays unheard
and hear what never is quite clear at sight.

CAROL OF A FATHER

He runs ahead to ford a flood of leaves—
he suddenly a forager and I
the lagging child content to stay behind
and watch the gold upheavals at the curb
submerge his surging ankles and subside.

A word could leash him back or make him turn
and ask me with his eyes if he should stop.
One word, and he would be a son again
and I a father sentenced to correct
a boy's caprice to shuffle in the drifts.

Ignoring fatherhood, I look away
and let him roam in his Octobering
to mint the memories of those few falls
when a boy can wade the quiet avenues
alone, and the sound of leaves solves everything.

FOR A SON WHO WILL NEVER BE BORN

When poplars spire stripped and brittle sticks
toward December stars, you will not see
the first ice catch and thicken at the curbs.
Balked of their first and last parenthesis,
the years will leave you winterless and free.

You will not know the exile's day, the nights
of thunder when the night is thunderless
and cloudless as the dark before your eyes,
nor will you grudge the waves of westering light
and the blood-bright sun ascending wonderless . . .

Less brave than Simeon, I speak my fear
for flesh not yet created, named, or known . . .
He blessed a child begotten crucified
and mocked with a prophecy all I would spare
you with these fostering, futile words, my son.

PARACHUTIST

After jump, drop, and somersault,
with cords unraveling in skein,
chute rising in a puff more taut
than sail until it domes a cone
of cords hooked to a harnessed dot
twirling and suspended like a toy
wind-swung and puppeted in space,
he pendulums sideways down the sky.

FOR A POET WHO WRITES AND WONDERS WHY

Because you are not what you will become
and cannot stop becoming what you are,
you never see that nothing but the lot
of being human summons you to write.

Perfect, you could know the world without a word.
Imperfect but perfectible, you must
unscroll your revelations line by line
to prove on paper what you sense at sight

as you are drawn to mirrors to confirm
that what you see reflected is yourself.
The need to be assured is nothing worse
than every poet's best apology.

Inspired, you must wait as consciously
as any actor playing dead on stage,
letting the world's quick purposes spin out
around you while you fidget with a thought

that will not let itself be brought to light
too easily or sooner than it must.
This much you owe to what the blood demands
but what the mind finds difficult to form

this side of Judgment where the mirror keeps
its darkness and the grave its victory.
Perfect as God, the final poetry
is silence, but that is still a death away.

GOD AND MAN

After casting the first act, checking sections
of scenery and mastering His rage
because the female lead blundered on page
one, He left the actors to themselves on stage
without a script and fretting for directions.

FOR MY LAST CLASS OF FRESHMEN

There is no word for what I love in you,
but it is sure, sacred and daily as bread.
I speak by indirections of a world
divisible as loaves among ourselves
and multiplied like miracles because
we share the private tables of the mind.
We join in rites and sacraments that bind

and keep us bound like vows when we face God
or Plato over coffee, books, and smoke.
Discovering the truth we always knew,
we look in one another's eyes surprised
and reconciled to what we shall recall
five years from now reclining on a plane,
exchanging socks, surrendering to pain,

dying, or saddleblocked before a birth.
Today it is enough that we rehearse
for nothing but today and everything
abreast of us impatient to be known.
If we profess no more but nothing less,
let us be tame as eagles, mad as saints,
or casual as Job in his complaints

until we learn the liturgies that sound
their psalms this second in the minstrel blood
alive from Solomon through Charlemagne
to Huckleberry's scuttlebutt to you.
Let us dare life as lovers dare the dark
and learn less stubbornly than blinded Saul
that light comes from within or not at all.

I make too much of it, this matter of books
and talk and silences, but every sun
I stand less sure of what I ought to know
and find my way to them to find my way.
Wisdom's rabbit races just far enough
ahead to keep the chase invitingly close
but never done, and all I really know
is what occurs to me right here as right.
Moments of truth come anywhere at once.

Facing the jewelry of bottles twiced
by mirrors fanned behind a downtown bar
in Minneapolis, I understood a verse
from Crane's *The Wine Menagerie* without
intending it. The meaning simply *came,*
like *that*—like one of God's gratuities
that come before we are prepared. Of all
I ever worked to learn, those things are best
that came to me without my earning them.

I should have said without *deserving* them.
In Minneapolis a deeper thinker
surely would have called all truth a gift,
but it was hot, and I forgot. Later,
when students let me tell them what I knew,
I saw that all we keep of truth is what
we give away, that holocausts can sleep
like revolutions in the smallest flints,
that any river can reflect the sun.

I have a student's fear that truth is fun
to seek but death to keep. Heroes and saints
are those who freed the thoughts of God by pen

or tongue and made them last like Parthenons.
I bleed the lambs of glory for those few
who said that time must wait their christening.
In the presence of their absence, words take flesh,
and God wakes fires that can rock the skull
and blaze the eye with revelation.

TRANSITION

A collar weighted with lieutenant's bars
made this a face to be saluted once
and possibly despised by one platoon
I marched ten miles in Norfolk fahrenheit.
Close-order-drill made me the martinet
I tried to tame, but Adam in my blood
inclined to epaulets until each stance
and striding flexed my sinews for command.

Soft holsters felt familiar at my hip,
and bayonets drove easily through groins
of dummies gallowed for the practice thrusts
like snakes impaled and twisting on a tine
to ready me for months of counting cash.
Released, I paid myself my vouchered sum
with bills that curved my wallet like a stave
and drove the pre-paid mileage into days

of typing theses in quintuplicate
and teaching boys the Latin ablative.
Surrendering my barracked ways meant more
than wearing out my military socks.
I kept a wry reservist's look for half
a year and still keep step with walkers-by,
although I hate the spectacle of squads
paced to a cadence in a drummed parade.

Between the sweep and sudden cease of grace
I wage today the quiet wars of art
with students calmly primed to probe my views
in lectures I cannot pre-think or plan.
I tell them only what I right now know.
I ask them only what they right now see
and take some triumph from each day's defeat
in my and everybody's war and peace.

GOAT-SONG

To bare the beast in flesh, the Greeks drew man
as satyr—waist-up human, waist-down brute.
Sculptors saw everywhere a twin of Pan,
each with the loins of a ram, some with a flute.
Not one concealed a hoof within a boot
or hid men's lowers in a business suit.
The Greeks, it seemed, preferred with rare exception
the worst distortion to the best deception.

TO A BICYCLIST IN FRANCE

For George James

You mail me postcards stamped in Paris—
Notre Dame illuminée, the ferried Seine,
the usual best-foot-forward city scenes.
Saying you miss the States, your words are pure

civilian now—all rank and rancor buried
with the notes you typed from B.O.Q.'s another
breed ago. You left the generals
their jeeps and crew-cuts for a biker's tour

of Europe on your saved-up pay, and shunned
the niche your father wanted you to fit . . .
The ex-lieutenant in me wakes and shakes
me ten years back. I could have biked from Caen,

have cashed my bonds and severance for fare
and pedaled humming through Montmartre, Versailles,
Provence, and downward to Marseille, but I
had someone else to be and somewhere next

to go with something there to do. My past
leaves Europe still mere names to me. At times
I have regrets—re-plot alternatives
I could have lived—pronounce my lived years lost . . .

Yet I can write without a hint of cant
I ride with you across the fact of France
as fast as I can think since thinking takes
me where I am despite these accidents

of place. Paris by night and Pittsburgh hills
are similarly still at 4:00 A.M.

Stillness is stillness, life is life, and earth
remains the earth with days quite short, and nights

shorter, and trips the shortest prank of chance.
Apart, we breathe this day alike and stand
an equal distance from eternity—
you there in the U.S.A., me here in France.

DYING UNDER DRILLING

Staring at a dentist's upside-down face, I tongue
the sand of pumice from my gums. "Rinse out."
I swill. "Open." I yawn like a baying wolf
at moons of frosted, incandescent bulbs.
More picks and clamps—a twang of snapping floss—
green spray that cools like winds of peppermint.
Beside me on a shelf, a skull—teeth clenched
in gumless glee or fury—hard to tell.
Who was this man? In heaven now, or hell?

When Hamlet stared at Yorick's dug-up grin,
did he consider anything beyond
mortality? Did he presume as I
assume that teeth are singular as souls
and fingerprints, that bodies burned to soot
can still be known as George or Josephine
by one identifying molar? Now,
updated by contraptions, I regress
to years when Mohawks practiced for distress

by letting chieftains hammer good bicuspids
out. In lesser anguish, David ordered
God to crush within their jaws the teeth
of all his enemies. But Mohawk guts
are dust with David's bones. Moldering now
like Hamlet stymied by a skull, I age
toward the buried Yorick I will be,
and, needled numb with darts of Novocain,
I fence with pain before the end of pain.

CIRCLING

Closer, I might see what water does
to rocks, and rocks to water—might read
the names of tugs diverging to the compass
points on Flushing Bay like gnats

across the skin of ponds. Instead,
I study cloudfoam and mountaintides
fogged in like cardboard country under
bunting. From twenty thousand feet

the Bronx conforms to abstract paintings
of the Bronx in atlases. Westward, Manhattan
sizzles like a grid of O's and X's
in a clash of tactics. Nearer, I might

scrutinize a tamer's lion gorged
with ox—drivers with lockjaw faces—
newsrack strippers showing this and that
to queues of browsers—books collapsing

on a shelf like sentinels who topple
from attention at attention. Stacked up
on this Olympus like a god, I see
no more than gray peninsulas and crisscross

roads. Round and around. No wonder
Zeus preferred sealevel living
to his alpy throne. Bollixed with altitude,
that old rapscallion's blood demanded

wenching in Salonika or sea-chilled wine
or anything to break his high monotony.
Divine or damned, the blood demands
a landing. Better to risk the earth

than drone in zeroes. Better to breathe
the grubby air where every day
is worth the waking. Godfather, show
me where to walk. I'll have to gamble

catching hell in heaven if I stumble.

TO A COMMENCEMENT OF SCOUNDRELS

My boys, we lied to you.
The world by definition stinks
of Cain, no matter what
your teachers told you. Heroes
and the fools of God may rise
like accidental green
on gray saharas, but the sand
stays smotheringly near.

Deny me if you can. Already
you are turning into personnel,
manpower, figures on a list
of earners, voters, prayers,
soldiers, payers, sums
of population tamed with forms:
last name, middle name, first name—
telephone—date of birth—

home address—age—hobbies—
experience. Tell them the truth.
Your name is Legion. You
are aged a million. Tell
them that. Say you breathe
between appointments: first day,
last day. The rest is no
one's business. Boys, the time

is prime for prophecy.
Books break down their bookends.
Paintings burst their frames.
The world is more than reason's
peanut. Homer sang it real.
Goya painted it, and Shakespeare
staged it for the pelting rinds
of every groundling of the Globe.

Wake up! Tonight the lions
hunt in Kenya. They
can eat a man. Rockets
are spearing through the sky.
They can blast a man to nothing.
Rumors prowl like rebellions.
They can knife a man. No one
survives for long, my boys.

Flesh is always in season,
lusted after, gunned, grenaded,
tabulated through machines,
incinerated, beaten to applause,
anesthetized, autopsied, mourned.
The blood of Troy beats on
in Goya's paintings and the truce
of Lear. Reason yourselves

to that, my buckaroos,
before you rage for God,
country, and siss-boom-bah!
You won't, of course. Your schooling
left you trained to serve
like cocksure Paul before
God's lightning smashed
him from his saddle. So—

I wish you what I wish
myself: hard questions
and the nights to answer them,
the grace of disappointment,
and the right to seem the fool
for justice. That's enough.
Cowards might ask for more.
Heroes have died for less.

SWIM

Behind my shoulders now
    the hanging moss of swings,
    popcorn, babies urinating
    through their bathing trunks,
    and dunes where couples later
    by the moon shall lie and lock
    in love's pretzel—.
                Seashore,
    I take leave of you for waves
    that surge like ink beyond
    the warning buoys.
                Farther,
    where the ink turns gray, turns
    green, turns purple to the sun,
    a submarine pumps out its bilges,
    veers and noses cleanly
    as a shark for Newport News.
Downcurrent, porpoises contort
    and gleam and vanish . . .
                There . . .

The combers ride behind
    me, ride and slacken
    back to surf and leave me be.
The lifeguard's whistle skips
    across the water like a stone,
    but I swim out and dare
    a cramp to knife me down
    to God.
                Later, I will seem
    the world's first fool,
    but now I judge myself
    by what I'm willing to survive
    without.
                The beach means nothing
    but a pound of folded clothing

checked for a chip I've rung
around my wrist.
                    Billfold,
keys to a door, the gathered
cards of my identity recede
like tides.
                  I'm just deadweight
bob-bobbing on the ballast
of my lungs that cannot choose
but float me eastward
from Virginia.
                 My fingerfaces
shrink with salt, but I
reach out for distance
and the time when all this sea
shall wear me down to man.
I want to crave each breath
   until I feel what breathing
means.
               My arms must ache,
my blood must burn before
I stroke ashore from outright
need and drop facedown
beneath the towel of the wind
and smell the sunset in a blanket.

CHILD OF OUR BODIES

Midway to birth, you are your own
secret. No one can tell me
how you'll be or when or where . . .

Not that the universe will change.
Suspended in the wombing air
where everything begins, the earth

keeps rolling on its ring from sun
to moon to sun again. I've sailed
the circle almost forty times,

but now your future makes me live
a different present than the one
I lived before you happened. Yes,

happened! After eleven years
my only precedent is silence.
I wait the justice of your eyes

exactly as I'm waiting now
for words to say what waiting means.
It does no good to school myself

for possibilities. Between
what never was and what shall be,
the only bravery is innocence.

BELLBEAT

The tongue of the bell must bang
    the bell's cold shell
    aloud to make the bell
    a bell.
           No otherwise exists.
What else is every iron
    peartop but an iron
    peartop if it simply cups
    its centered stamen still?
The frozen pendulum strikes
    nil.
       It plumblines
down like double hands
    made one at half past six.
I've seen the carilloning
    tulips battened down
    in belfries.
           I've heard them
rock and creak in rainy
    winds.
         I've felt the dangled
nubs inch close to sound
    but never close enough
    before the muting night
    enshrines them in their brass
    monotony.
         It takes the tugging
down and easing up
    on one lowknotted rope
    to jell the shape and sound
    of what remembers to become
    a bell.
        And gong it goes,
it goes, it goes . . .
And tones go sheeping over,
    after, under one

another, shuddering in high
   cascades from quick to quiet.
The muffled bellbeat
   in my chest rhymes every
   beat of the bell with breath.
It tolls my seven circles
   in the sun.
                It thunders in my
   wrists.
            It does not rest.

LOST SWIMMER

Each poem I surprise from hiding
    is a face I learn to draw
    by drawing it.
                    Masterplan?
None.
        Strategy?
                    None except
    whatever wits I pit
    against myself to bring it
    off.
            Never the face
    imagined nor a face in fact,
    my making is its own solution.
It tells me how it must
    become, and I obey or else.
I see myself as some
    lost swimmer of the night
    who must discover where
    he goes by going.
                    Uncertain,
    dared and curious, I stall
    my dive until the surface
    stills its saucered ditto
    of the moon.
                Then, plunge . . .
Sleep's inland waves lock over
    me.
        Ashore, the sealevel
    world of pistols, porkchops,
    mirrors, and garbage ripens
    into headlines.
                But where I
    plummet, horses ride on wings,
    water burns, and willows

write their reasons in the wind.
The pure imagination of a dream
   is mine to swim until
   the baiting light betrays
   me.
      And I rise.
              The shore
steadies where I left it.
                   The whole
unfloatable and failing world
goes by as given.
           I swim
from maybe to the merely real
and make them one with words.
I wonder how I did
   it.
      I wondered how I'll do
   it.
      And I've done it.

VOODOO

Profession?
                Wordsmith.
                            Ambition?
Only to leave American
    no worse because I wrote it.
Failings?
                Truculence beyond
reason.
            Tell me I can't
be disappointed and believe,
and, disappointed, I'll go on
believing.
                Suggest I roam
for inspiration, and I'll say
the knife I hone in my own
room would cut no keener
in Japan, Geneva, or the Hebrides.
Call poetry the voodoo of the mad,
    and I'll explain how madness
    keeps me sane.
                        Better mad
than futile.
                    Defenses?
                            Search
me, and you'll find no
loaded automatic hidden
in my pocket like pornography, no
shield except an aging
epidermis fuzzed with hair,
no tactic but the ruse of trust.
Results?
            Who knows?
                        It's still
the price of love to fight
the battle for the future now

and lose.
At least I know
what I'll say no or yes to
long before I must.
Meanwhile,
I stay a breath away
from God and write down what
I just remember.
A word here . . .
A phrase there . . .
Not much
to memorize unless a consecration
comes to make them worth
remembering.
But if and where
it comes, then watch me stitch
my dreams to syllables, connive
with pens like some magician
in a frenzy, shake to hell
this seven-come-eleven world,
and make what's happening my heaven.

SKYCOAST

I'd build a house with windows
  in the roof so I could see
  from underneath the plunge
  and spatter of rain, snow
  in a bluster, hail hitting . . .
Having a skycoast would
  liven me more than living
  near the sea.
            No sound.
                    No
smell.
      No villainy.
                  Air
is my element.
            Its pitch
and pressure keep me
as and what I am.
No one can drown in it.

Skull of a bull . . .
                    Whitening,
        the bone turns conjurer
        to recollect the steer who mounted
        cows in utter boredom,
        hoofed through dung, and butted
        in brute fury the caping
        flies.
            Gored by the horn
        of truth, I heed what hides
        in smithereens.
                    What am
        I but a smithereen myself?
Among all past and present
        images of God, I live
        complete but still a part
        of what the integer of me
        completes.
                    Trillions remain
        divisible by me.
                    Raise
        me to any power possible,
        and I identify myself
        in multiples of everyone
        and anywhere.
                    Fragment
        by fragment, I piece my own
        mosaic of the world.
                    Soaring
        over Lesbos, I remember all
        that's left of Sappho's oracles.
Like crumbs of rock I swiped
        from the Acropolis, her talismans
        unbury Greece.
                    Shepherds

flock their ewes.
                    A lover
flexes in a hug of thighs
to seed from scratch our first
mythologies.
                    What more is
mating but a match of fractions?
What afterlock of loins
    shelled Venus from the sea
    or posed her naked on de Milo's
    pedestal?
                    Intact, her torso
    breeds no mystery.
                    Only
    the arms that are not there
    are there for anyone's imagining,
    and armlessly she beckons us.
In time and out of time
    she hunts me to my last
    division.
                    Is she God's virgin
    or the bitch of trumps?
                            In punctual
    Geneva she awakens me
    while pigeons chortle back
    the night, inching the morning
    on until it candles
    everywhere at once.
Near Evian she plays Pandora
    to the wind and harps the pinwheel
    spokes of bikers into hymns . . .
In Istanbul the immemorial,
    she chants a thought of Harry
    dying in the States.
                            "Poems

create what prose is left
to talk about."
                    In Sariyer,
Daglarca finishes what Harry
meant.
          "Poems are letters
from our closest friends."
                    In Turkish
or American, these prophecies
deliver me.
                    I hammer ashes
from my pipe and sow them
where the continents divide
Byzantium.
                    The sutures of the earth
will never close, and ashes
resurrect the dragon's teeth
of fear.
                    A submarine from Russia
splits the Bosphorus.
                    From home
the talk is politics and guns.
A tongue inside the facts
announces to the wind what
every poet knows.
                    The rest
is history.
                    The rest is prose.

MY ROOSEVELT COUPÉ

Coax it, clutch it, kick it
   in the gas was every dawn's
   scenario.
           Then off it bucked,
   backfiring down the block to show
   it minded.
            Each fender gleamed
   a different hue of blue.
Each hubcap chose
   its hill to spin freewheeling
   into traffic.
            I fretted like a spouse
   through chills and overboiling,
   jacked my weekly flats,
   and stuffed the spavined seats
   with rags.
            Leaking, the radiator
   healed with swigs of Rinso,
   brake fluid, and rainwater.
              Simonized,
   the hood stuck out like a tramp
   in a tux.
           All trips were dares.
Journeys were sagas.
           From Norfolk
   to New York and back,
   I burned eleven quarts
   of oil, seven fuses,
   and the horn.
           One headlight
   dimmed with cataracts.
             The other
   funneled me one-eyed
   through darker darks than darkness . . .
O my Roosevelt coupé, my first,

my Chevrolet of many scars
and heart attacks, where are you
now?
            Manhandled, you'd refuse
to budge.
                  Stickshifted
into low, you'd enigmatically
reverse.
            Sold finally
for scrap, you waited on your treads
while I pocketed thirty
pieces of unsilver and slunk
away—Wild Buck Hazo
abandoning his first and favorite
mount, unwilling to malinger
long enough to hear
the bullet he could never fire.

THE JACKS

Booted to the knees in brass,
    I stomp through dreams.
                    My feet
are penances.
            Snow freezes
to my eyeskins, and my lashes
lock.
       Under the grunts
of guns, my son, my son
keeps calling me.
               I stumble
over swamps of sleep until
my room explodes its beaches
in my face . . .
           Midnight.
                  My wife,
my Anne, sleeps at my right.
My son kicks down his sheet
    and yawns his eyebrows to a frown.
Numb from nightmare, I hide
    behind the days I've lived,
    poems made, miles
    driven, students known.
The inventory chokes.
             Terror's
ace still plays the king.
The spades of death stay
    shuffled in the deck.
             Facedown
they come.
          The dealer's blind.
I draw the jacks I am.
Father.
    Poet.
        Born

jokers both . . .

                They stake
me through the poker of my days.
Against the night's full
    house, what can I
    bid?
        I play for time,
  time, time.
            No one can
pass.
      Winner takes all,
and the spades, the spades are wild.

Down on my knees and palms
   beside my son, I rediscover
   doormats, rugnaps,
   rockerbows, and walljoints
   looming into stratospheres
   of ceiling.
             A telephone
  rings us apart.
               I'm plucked
  by God's hooks up
  from Scylla through an open door,
  Charybdis in a socket, and a Cyclops
  lamp that glares floorlevel
  souls away from too much
  light to lesser darknesses.
What god in what machine
   shall pluck my son?
              Amid
  the Carthage of his toys, he waits
  unplucked, unpluckable.
                 I

  gulliver my way around
  his hands and leave him stalled
  before the Matterhorn of one
  of seven stairs.
             Floorbound,
  he follows, finds and binds
  my knees with tendrils of receiver
  cord.
          I'm suddenly Laocoön
  at bay, condemned to hear
  some telephoning Trojan offer
  me a more prudential life
  where I can wake insured
  against disaster, sickness, age,

and sundry acts of Genghis
God.
                    Meanwhile, I'm slipping
tentacles and watching my
confounding namesake toddle free . . .
Bloodbeats apart, he shares
with me the uninsurable air.
We breathe it into odysseys
where everyone has worlds to cross
and anything can happen.
Like some blind prophet
cursed with truth, I wish
my son his round of stumbles
to define his rise.
                         Nothing
but opposites can ground him
to the lowest heights where men
go, lilliputian but redeemable.
Before or after Abraham,
what is the resurrection and the life
except a father's word
remembered in his son?
                         What more
is Isaac or the Lord?
                         Breath
and breathgiver are one, and both
are always now as long
as flesh remembers.
                         No
testament but that lives on.
The torch of blood is anyone's
to carry.
              I say so as my son's
father, my father's son.

A SECOND DARK

I am my son listening
   to me, drinking the rhymes
   my lips shall never unremember,
   watching the ceiling dance
   with dreams.
               The moon stays where
   I name it.
         My kite sleeps
   in a tree as surely as my blue
   pajamas end in socks.
I hear me telling me
   how whales fly through
   the sea, how sparrows swim
   the wind, and why the sun
   burns down.
              Never so nimble
   as Jack nor simple as Simon
   nor quick as Cinderella's prince,
   I let my stories ramble me
   from dark to dark.
             We reach
   the dark of separate sleep
   and then a second dark where
   I become my son, myself,
   my father all at once . . .
             Softly,
   my pillow mothers me
   almost asleep, almost . . .
It's time again.
        My son
 tosses through his own tonight.
I grow into the forty years,
   eight months, and twenty
   days of me.
        Who drifted

islands of oystercrackers
soddenly in gumbo?
                    Who lighted
epitaphs in transit and bent
the bending candleflames
to silence with a single breath?
The day's last coffee
cools in my cup while I
suck pipesmoke.
                    Mouths
on television reveille the dying
living room with taps.
I sip, puff, doze.
Dreams of the world bleed by.

THE DARKER NOON

We sail asleep from midnight
    to a beach named dawn.
You stir.
        I wake.
                My only
stars are latitudes.
                Tomorrow
is a shore we may not reach,
so let it wait.
                Raccoons
are floating in their hollow
oak cocoons.
                A milkman
boats his bottles.
                The last
buses trundle to their docks
across the tire-stenciled snow.
Marking the darker noon
    of the clock, the dual arrows
fuse into a mast that tolls
    through silence to the first birds.
The seabell of a siren wakens
    you.
                My wife.
                    My mate.
Let all the klaxons clang.
These temporary sheets
    are jetsam to the moon.
                    How love
makes one what life keep two
is where we are and when.
No ports.
                No bo's'ns but ourselves.
No echo but the wake we make
    to show we buccaneered that sea.

45

THREE MADE ONE

The roof reverberates with trills
and paradiddles of the rain.
                              Shelled
in the shelling car, we are three
made one against the weather.
My son wipes portholes
on the window fog and looks
for submarines.
                         Watercolors
of Ohio cross the rainshield:
cows in a phalanx, tails
to the wind, heads huddled,
pelts draining.
                    From nowhere
soars a rainbow.
                    The grass
bristles and glistens to the sun's
revenge.
              The elms shake out
their leaves.
              A cow dries
brighter than a toweled calf.
But the rainbow . . .
                         My bride
glows in blue silver.
Russet defines my son.
                         Tomorrow
I'll remember this as I remember
ship shapes of French fries,
coffee in Egypt, Caracas
from a cablecar . . .
                         Memory's bad
checks buy nothing back.
Ahead is where the rainbow
shines.

I tell my boy we're
heading underneath the arch
of all that color.
                    Even when
it fades, I tell him that.

QUARTERED

Beneath my room's square
   sky, I grow like fog
   into the room's corners.
I read each window's page
   of frost, assume the aristocracy
   of walls, populate space.
Knowing the boy within me
   dead, the man dying,
   I swallow whole
   what boxes me.
               Inside the room
inside myself, I multiply
   to four.
        One *me* keeps
siding with himself.
            A second
lives for death to hide
   from living.
          A third believes
he's everyone.
        A fourth
demands his heaven now.
Alone with opposites, I wait
   sequestered like a portrait,
   framed.
       I want to break
the frame.
        My four identities
won't have it.
        Suspended
from their compass points, I am
my own apocalypse whom four
brute horses try to pull
asunder.
       They leave me holding
on, holding my bones
together.
      Still holding.

THE FIRST AND ONLY SAILING

Your shores diminish.
                    You learn
    the doom of sailors drifting
    south on ice islands.
What echoes shall you code
    to float the sea?
                    When Manolete
    got it from Islero in Linares,
    he rose again as four
    stone matadors in Córdoba.
Likewise Philippe-Auguste,
    who paid his bodyguards with whores
    to keep them loyal.
                    This side
    of memory, you fight the killing
    tides to death for etchings
    on a rock, for life.
                    As for
    the Happy Isles?
                    Let dreamers
    dock there.
                    Believe in such,
    and you'll believe that Essex,
    More, and Mary of Scotland
    kidded the chopper on their climb
    to God.
                    Settle for the whirlpool
    and the cliff.
                    Mermaidens, naked
    at the nipples and below, still
    mate with sailors in their sleep.
And who escapes from sleep?
Waken, and you wage one ship
    against the aces of the sea.
Weaken, and the bait of Faust's bad

wager waits you.
                    Worsen,
and the winds of old indulgence
overtake you.
                    You face them
as you'd face, years afterward,
a girl you kissed and fondled
in a park but never married.
Becalmed, you make your peace
    with dreams.
                    Expect nothing,
and anything seems everything.
Expect everything, and anything
    seems nothing . . .
                    To live
you leave your yesterselves
to drown without a funeral.
You chart a trek where no
    one's sailed before.
                    You rig.
You anchor up.
                    You sail.

SPLITTING

Unchanged: my whiskersnow of salt
    and pepper in the sink, the shaver
    shearing my chill cheek warm,
    a palmweight of buzzering.
                            With half
    my face to do, a higher power
    sizzles my razor mute.
                        Only
    my passport knows me now.
My mirror shows me half-American,
    half-Adam . . .
                        Beyond my balcony
    all Zurich rises to a signature
    of skyline.
                    Half here, half home,
    half shaven, half asleep, I could be
    watching Cairo, Istanbul, Madrid,
    Beirut.
                A pigeon waves goodbye
    with both its wings and swerves
    for France.
                    My western stare
    outflies it to the Spanish coast,
    the sea and, all at once,
    the States, the States!
                        What is it
    to be gone but never gone?
What leaves me more American
    in Zurich than in Pennsylvania?
For answers I might interview
    those voyagers who've docked with God
    or be myself in different
    hemispheres at once.
                        The Tartars

understood.
                    Away from home,
they kept their jackboots double-soled
with China's soil—so, no matter
where they walked, they walked on China.

ANTICIPATING YESTERDAY, REMEMBERING
TOMORROW

A white stern-wheeler slides
    downriver for Ohio.
                            Its paddles
    plow the river rough until
    they seem to falter and reverse.
I've seen the same illusion
    in the backward-spinning tires
    of a car accelerating forward,
    props revolving clockwise
    counterclockwise, trains departing
    from a town departing from a train
    departing.
                    To break the spell,
    I focus on the stern-wheel's hub
    and slide into a memory of Paris . . .
At Notre Dame a life
    I seemed to know preceded me.
On Montparnasse I told myself
    I must have come that way
    before I came that way.
No matter where I walked,
    I kept retreating into what
    came next.
                    Even the Seine
    deceived me with its waves blown
    east, its current coasting west . . .
The wheel I watch keeps wheeling
    me behind, ahead, around.
I clench my lashes to the wind
    and wait.
                    When I release,
    I know a place I've never seen.
I see a time I've known

forever.
　　　　Is it tomorrow, yesterday,
today?
　　　　I drink a breath.
I breathe my life away.

TOASTS FOR THE LOST LIEUTENANTS

For Karl the Cornell rower,
    who wore the medals he deserved.
For Grogan of Brooklyn, who left
    no memory worth mentioning.
For Foley, who married the commandant's
    daughter though nothing came of it.
For Clasby, who wanted out,
    and when he could, got out.
For Schoen, who married, stayed in,
    thickened, and retired a major.
For Chalfant, who bought a sword
    and dress blues but remained Chalfant.
For Billy Adrian, the best
    of punters, legless in Korea.
For Nick Christopolos, who kept
    a luger just in case.
For Soderberg, who taught us
    songs on the hot Sundays.
For Dahlstrom, the tennis king,
    who starched his dungarees erect.
For Jacobson, who followed me
    across the worst of all creeks.
For Laffin and the gun he cracked
    against a rock and left there.
For Nathan Hale, who really was
    descended but shrugged it off.
For Elmore, buried in Yonkers
    five presidents ago.
For Lonnie MacMillan, who spoke
    his Alabamian mind regardless.
For Bremser of Yale, who had *it*
    and would always have *it*.
For lean Clyde Lee, who stole
    from Uncle once too often.
For Dewey Ehling and the clarinet

he kept but never played.
For Lockett of the Sugar Bowl
   champs, and long may he run.
For Lyle Beeler, may he rot
   as an aide to the aide of an aide.
For Joe Buergler, who never
   would pitch in the majors.
For Kerg, who called all women cows
   but married one who wasn't.
For me, who flunked each
   test on weapons but the last.
For Sheridan, who flunked them all,
   then goofed the battle games
   by leaving his position, hiding
   in a pine above the generals'
   latrine until he potted
   every general in sight, thus
   stopping single-handedly the war.

FOR V AFTER Z

Tyrants ago, you would have had
    your tongue sliced off, your fingers
    crushed, your wife indentured,
    and your name disgraced.
                       Today
you simply can't go home.
What's left but Paris, West
    Berlin, Vienna, Rome?
Remember when we talked Cavafy
    while our coffees clouded
    with goatcream and triple sugars?
One poet was afoot and reading
    what was Greek to both of us
    and still sounds Greek to me.
The news was Esso and a king.
The Yankee fleet in port
    behaved like any fleet in port.
"Happy the nation," wrote Montesquieu,
    "whose annals of history are dull."
Dullness swam in our coffee
    as we toasted time to write
    and do that well, love one wife
    and do that better, live
    as witnesses and do that best.
We toasted everyone but undermen
    and fearers of the word.
                When these
    prevailed along with soldiers,
    censors, millionaires, and chosen
    churchmen, toasts became
    seditious as a song or syllable.
Because you praised a countryman
    who heeded pulses with his fingertips,

you got the boot.
                        The charge?
Spreading fire, asking
    questions, jarring the faith
    of true believers.
                        The sentence?
Exile.
        Not quite so bad
    as watching vultures peck your liver,
    drinking hemlock, or deserving
    feces on your grave, but punishment
    enough . . .
                        Tonight, for what
    it's worth, let's say that Montesquieu
    was right.
                        Dull days might
    come again when witnesses
    can toast their coffee cold,
    and only poetry is dangerous.

DON JUAN'S DREAM OF NEAR AND FAR MISSES

Your wenching done, you dreamed
   alive your score of paramours:
   she with the whore's lips, she
   from the shore, she with the tanned
   hips, she with real panthers
   staring from her eyes, she
   of the whips and mirrors . . .
                       All
   these you numbered to your skills
   like scalps or notches on a rifle
   stock or stenciled emblems
   of the sun across a fuselage.
Was every girl herself
   or what you dreamed she was?
In Montreal she whispered no,
   no, no, no, no.
                  In Alexandria
   she plucked her eyebrows in the nude.
In Rome she never gave
   her name.
             Each time you found
   and took her, she became herself
   anew in someone else.
                  Was she
   Yvonne, who never kissed by day,
   or Evelyn, who tangoed you to death?
And what of the twins from Spain?
You offered Ava Eva's ring
   engraved with Eva's name
   and Ava's anniversary.
               When trouble
   doubled, you resolved to choose
   the mate who'd save you from yourself.
Docile you would have her, schooled
   in deference, religious to a point
   but not averse to dalliance.

She of the king's inheritance?
Already spoken for . . .
                        She
without attachments?
                        Dying
in Lugano . . .
                        She who had called
you casual?
                        Your letter came back
burned . . .
                        At last the Home for Old
Lotharios admitted you.
                        Nuns
assisted you with slippers, pills,
and liniments.
                        You saw fresh
universes in their faces, not two
the same but all beyond you.
By night you learned again
    that loins were loins.
                        Blinder
than revenge, they made their own
decisions.
                        You showered in ice water,
practiced Zen, saltpetered
all your meals.
                        Hair-shirted
in your cell, you vowed before
the god of all lost loves
that you would never take
that road again, that you
would take that road never
again, that you would take never
that road again.
                        Halfway down
the road, you kept repeating that.

THE JOHNSTOWN FLY

November's in his wings.
                    He hovers
    aft and low without a whirr
    like some leftover Messerschmitt
    from all the wars of August.
A Gideon Bible, cleft to Nehemiah,
    subs as runway.
                    He lands
    between verse twenty and the gutter.
Seven times seven times I stalk
    him with a Johnstown phonebook
    as my swatter.
                    Miss by miss
    I mock him as a flyweight
    bum no longer ranked but sly
    enough to keep from being bopped.
He bounces off the ropes, stays close,
    turns cagey in the clinches, goes
    the distance, thumbs his nose
    at all my blasphemy, and earns
    a draw.
                    That settled, he walks
    a wall to heaven and retires
    for life.
                When I demand
    a rematch, he resumes the buzzing
    status of his kind . . .
                        In Nehemiah's
    era, flies outnumbered armies.
During the Johnstown flood,
    the flies stayed dry.
                    And in
    the world of words, flies *are*
    what planes and eagles merely *do* . . .
Unflappable, this fly presumes
    that history will make me seek

a truce.
It does.
I do.
We call it quits like champions
in separate divisions.
He's
satisfied.
I'm satisfied.

ON THE METROLINER I REMEMBER THAT TO BE IS TO REMEMBER

Passing mountains of crushed cars,
    I realize my kingdom's gone.
Behind me stay the streets
    of triple-bolted doors, dog
    waste, and armed custodians.
Double-paneled windows
    filter out New Jersey's smog
    while Muzak's cushion music
    gasses me asleep.
                I wake
    to non-America.
              The badge
  is hair.
       The code is noise.
Barreling through Trenton, I count
    karate parlors by the fives.
Bumper stickers blare
    the new theology.
             I want
    to swallow snow and drink
    rain, tell pollsters I'm my own
    majority, reread the lives
    of Lincoln and Geronimo.
                    Who cares?
The crowd still wants Barabbas
    while the crowd's evangelist and Mr.
    Anybody marry God and Caesar
    on prime time.
             Shepherds have
  sheep's heads and sheep's habits.
Central Unintelligence insults
    intelligence.
             Unfree unlove
  is for dogs . . .

When was it
any better?
                        Any worse?
                                    With
countrymen who can't not win
and seldom question, questions
are a fool's profession.
                              Still,
I question.
                  Between what used to be
New York and what's no longer
Philadelphia, I resurrect Diogenes.
My seat becomes the tub
    I sleep in.
                    My overcoat's my blanket,
and my roof's the sky.
                            To every
Alexander on the march, I send
condolences and bone dust.
                                  To all
who ask me where I think I'm going,
I answer that I'm going where I think.
And as for finding one just man
    to prove that justice still
    is possible?
                    I'll take the brightest
lantern on the brightest morning
of the brightest summer of the almanac
and look and look and look.

BREAKFASTING WITH SOPHOMORES

When I was what you are, the world
   was every place I'd yet to go.
Nothing near, now, or here
   meant more than something anywhere
   tomorrow.
              Today, the ratio's reversed.
Back from anywhere, I watch
   the Indiana earth I walked,
   measure Indiana's level weathers
   and remember . . .
              Where did twenty-five
Decembers go?
          North of action,
   east of indecision, south
   of possibility, and west of hope,
   I stare into the now and then
   of all those years at once.
A sophomore who has my name jogs
   by in ski boots and an army-surplus
   jacket.
        Netless tennis courts
   turn populous with players only
   I can recognize.
          Oblivious,
   the campus pines still celebrate
   their rooted anniversaries.
            A DC-7
   seams the zenith with a chalkmark
   wake, and clouds rush over
   lake, dome, and stadium
   like bursts of smoke from field
   artillery . . .
          No different in its bones,
   no greener, not a foot more hilly,

Indiana's real for the acknowledging.
I sit back, listening, observing,
    memorizing everything.
Two decades' worth
    of meals and months and mileage
    consecrates this minute.
                    Even
an eyelash swimming in my coffee
seems important.
                When I was half
my age, I never would have seen it.

RADIUS

Salted by rain, the ocean
    roughens into clashing circles.
They widen, arc by arc,
    toward predictable collisions
    with the shores.
                After they shatter,
    you remember you're the core of every
    circle that begins with you.
Like any hub, you center
    six-times-sixty spokes
    that finger outward for the poles,
    the centuries, the stars.
                You intersect
    a candled dinner at the Ritz,
    the oiled sculpture of a riflestock
    against a hunter's shoulder,
    hummingbirds blown wild as ashes
    in a hurricane.
                If poetry is traveling
    without a ticket, you're a poet.
You follow every radius
    as far as you can dream.
             No
    matter where your body's been
    or where it goes or what
    it leaves you to remember, all
    your dreams precede you . . .
Before the astronauts, you left
    your bootprints on the moon.
Predating all the conquerors, you saw
    the cedars of the Lord.
             The way
    you danced through Paris in your sleep
    makes Paris dance that dream
    awake each time you summer there.
Fulfilling all your prophecies

by running into them, you're like
the bull's-eye of a world within
a world around a core that opens
in the always present to the never
very far.
　　　　When you stand still,
you're one of many radiating suns
until the air becomes the sum
of circles interlocked like zeros
on the sea.
　　　　　　Each circle's center
never moves.
　　　　　　　Each center's circles
never stop.
　　　　　To be both one
and all is what they teach you.
Wait, and the rings will reach you.

AN AMERICA MADE IN PARIS

1. SIGNING THE AIR

You dream you've used this tool
      for sixty years.
                  Even Pablo
      liked the way it left your signature
      in fissures that denied your fingers.
All your bronze or marble sculptures
      grew from clay.
                  You told Picasso,
      "Ruiz, if slime was adequate
      for God, then clay is adequate
      for me."
                  Paint was his clay.
Blue paint was all he could
      afford in that cold "period"
      near Sacre-Coeur.
                  Instead
      of models, Pablo posed some
      Montmartre whores to be
      Les Demoiselles d'Avignon.
Whores were cheap for men who pooled
      their francs and lived for months
      on sweet potatoes, leeks,
      and long, stale loaves.
You called yourselves the wards
      of Paris.
                  But so did everyone:
      Armenians, monarchists, expatriates
      like Joyce, Americans who came
      to find America in France
      and did and wrote it down
      in books and took it home
      with them.
                  No matter where
      you went from Montparnasse to Rue

Lepic, something was happening.
Each Sunday, Hemingway would stop
    or Nadia Boulanger with Archie
    and Ada MacLeish or Ezra Pound
    with his cane.
                        Rodin patrolled
    the Tuileries beside his aide—
    a German-Czech named Rilke.
Modigliani painted and repainted
    the same unsmiling icon
    with the breasts of Venus.
                        For you,
    each model was a midnight bride.
Her name was Fun-without-a-face
    or Headache-in-the-morning.
                        After
    you found the one whose life meant
    more to you than yours, the slightest
    infidelity was like the mating
    of hyena with hyena.
                        All
    you remembered was the smell.
Married or unmarried, Pablo
    never understood.
                        A Mediterranean
    of the Spanish earth, he kept
    his minotaur erect until the end . . .
Then, *fini!*
                        Your final day
    in Paris dawned no different
    than your first.
                        Croissants
    and cheeses from Gruyere . . .
                            The sun's
    a coppery shower.

You sip
black coffee.
You trace meandering
rivers of grain around
two knotholes in the tabletop.
Across the Seine, the Eiffel
Tower interrupts the sky.
The blue
south steadies the gray
north over Notre Dame.
You
swallow coffee like the sacrament.
The panorama's like a canvas
with the paints still moist.
You squint it into focus, smile,
and sip as if the only thing
still left to do is fit
that sacred city in a frame,
then pencil in the lower right-
hand corner—very small—your name.

2.   THE VIGIL

See?
Of course, you see, see well,
see better than most.
But seeing's
not enough.
You're like the boy
who had no courage but the courage
of his eyes to say the naked
emperor was naked after all.
You paint what you see until

71

you see what the paint sees.
Some painters build their paintings.
You discover yours when they
    discover you.
                    Most nights
you sit before an empty
canvas like a guard on post,
deciding what you just won't
do.
        That's all that painting
means to you: deciding what
is worth the paint or not.
Perusing Schiele's sketches or Picasso's,
    you learn their art from what
    they both left out.
                    Cézanne?
No different.
                    Hemingway learned
leanness from Cézanne, and Hemingway
stayed lean as veal.
                    You nix
experience.
                    Experience deceived
Renoir.
        The two-sweet pink of all
those tubbed and tubby bottoms
sweetened with the years . . .
                            Gauguin
drew better as he aged.
                    You taste
his greens and browns.
                    Dali?
An average draftsman but a clown
    at heart.
            Compared with Goya,
he's a speck.

Utrillo drafted,
but he drafted with God's eye.
And Schiele?
                His crazyquilts of hell
and all those models—drawn
as if their pubises were mouths—
were masterpieces from the start.

3. SOME WORDS FOR PRESIDENT WILSON

Declaring war on Germany but not
    its citizens, he took no enemy
    for granted but Americans.
                        They
    crippled him.
                    After his stroke
    he somehow kept his grin.
                        That,
    his pince-nez and his Presbyterian
    chin survived the lost
    election and the sag of normalcy.
Blanketed and read to by a wife
    rare men deserve, he thought
    of Princeton, Trenton, and the years
    before Versailles . . .
                        He never guessed
    that he would be the final
    President to write his speeches
    out by hand.
                    Or that
    the future he foresaw but never
    saw would happen differently
    the same and change its wars
    by number, not by name.

4. NAPOLEON'S

Appropriate that near the tomb
    of Bonaparte, upended cannon
    barrels should defend the corridors.
This Corsican who loved artillery
    would surely have condoned such vigilance.
"Give them a whiff of grape,"
    he muttered once before he fired
    at a mob with scattershot.
                        To crack
    an enemy's defense he nixed
    direct assaults as rapes.
                        Instead,
    he concentrated all his cannonpower
    on the weakest of the weakest flanks
    of that defense until it cracked.
Accepting losses with a lover's
    shrug, he claimed that Paris
    could replace them in a single night.
At Waterloo, the rain, not Wellington,
    defeated him.
                        Unable to maneuver
    caissons in the mud, he damned
    the French, the English, and himself
    to history.
                        That history engraves
    the upright cannonshaft that he
    erected in the Place Vendomê
    from all the melted guns of Austerlitz.
Centering the square, it scrolls
    in corkscrew chapters to its tip
    a bronze procession of the passionate
    in arms . . .
                        Outside the Ritz,
    a newsgirl pedals by, her nipples

tenting a *Herald-Tribune*
T-shirt sweated to her breasts.
Tour guides and all the guided near
    the pillar glance away from France
    to study what is after all
    quite clearly in a manner of speaking
    also a piece of the tale of France.
Aroused and rising to a war
    they think they'll win, a few
    stragglers, squinting at their target's
    front and flanks, change
    suddenly to cannoneers and zero in.

5.   WHITE SILENCE

You work more slowly now.
It's not the years.
                    It's
    how the years insist on being
    kept in mind that tires you.
You sit in death's lap and know it.
Years back, you imitated Georges
    Rouault, painting sundowns
    in the morning.
                    Now you reach
    for noons at midnight, and they're gone.
But still you reach . . .
                    Beyond
    your window you can see a pair
    of helicopters snoop like dragonflies
    for traffic clots.
                    A bird-chalked
    general goes on commanding
    from his rusting saddle.

Vapor shimmies
from the manhole lids like steam
from old volcanoes.
                    You'd love
to paint the silence there.
                    Impossible?
No more impossible than making maps
or sketching nudes.
                    What else
are maps but studies in abstraction?
Whoever saw the earth from those
     perspectives?
                    Who christened Europe
green and Asia blue?
                    And as
for nudes, what are they but
complexities of light and lines?
You catch the light by painting in
     the lines.
                    Later, you erase the lines.
You feel the silence of the street
     that way.
                    You've walked those stones
so many times they talk to you.
You listen with your heels.
                    If you
could solve—if you could only
solve that silence with a brush . . .
To see is not enough.
                    You've seen
too much already, and you don't
     forget.
                    You even notice how
the recto-verso greens of dollars
reproduce the tails and heads

of maple leaves.
                    Half your
life is learning to express
that kind of trivial amazement.

6.   ELEGY FOR THE FIRST LIFE

Without your mate, you learned
    that love's the only cancer.
It kills by not killing.
You kept your attic stocked
    with what you chose together:
    pewter salad spoons, pepper grinders
    carved from sandalwood,
    suede scraps, and railroad calendars.
Her favorite was a bathtub squared
    on four bronze claws.
You trucked it from Versailles
    for her.
                    Its porcelain peeled
    and cracked as small as puzzle pieces
    or as large as separate states.
For years you mopped and swept
    and locked the attic like a shrine.
Your mopcords tufted down
    into a spinster's knot.
                    The broomstraw
    slanted from a thousand sweeps
    until you swung the handle
    like a hockey stick . . .
                    Once,
    even the dust was important.

7.   WAITING FOR ZERO

Confirming that the avant-garde
    can't wait for history, gray Hemingway
    reached Paris seven days before
    the Liberation.
               With Nazis near
    the Place Vendomê, he freed
    his moveable feast and waited
    for the troops . . .
                 Like Hemingway you wait
    for snow before a January second
    masquerading as the first of May.
The maple buds almost believe it.
Stallion dung around a pear tree
    thaws into its pasture smell
    again.
          Even a buried crocus
    lets its periscope break ground.
So far, no snow.
          Whether
    it will come or go is in
    the winds of Canada.
             But you . . .
You act as if it's here.
             Your blood's
    already down to three below.
Your shoulders chill and heighten
    in the winds to come.
             Remembering
    the future as a fact, you turtle up
    like any seed beneath the snow
    or like a snoozing black bear
    in the hills and wait for Easter,
    wait for history . . .
             But just suppose
    the wait's too long and troublesome.

Or else suppose that Easter's
    not enough—or not at all.
Which brings you back to Hemingway
    in Idaho in 1961.
                    His feast
no longer moveable, his hunter's
eyes too sick to see, his future
certain to grow worse, he faced
the choice of waiting for the end
or not.
            At last he thought
ahead of how it felt to be
the first to Paris.
                Then,
he held the muzzle cold
between his teeth and bit and shot.

8.   THE LONG PASSION

Your paintings show us all
    born crucified.
                Christian
or Jew, there's no denying that.
Accepting it is something else.
Accepting it and going on
    is something more.
                    You can't
call any man a man
who hasn't seen the nailmarks
in his palms.
            Religious?
                    No.
You quit on planned religions
    when you learned to doubt.
                        If   79

praying in a pew meant asking
God to guarantee salvation
in advance, you saw all praying
as a bet, with God the pot . . .
For you a life to come must equal
living at the peak and then
exceed it.
                    If not, why live
to die?
              When you were young,
you prayed and fasted for the truth
until you understood why Protestants
go mad, and Catholics sin,
and Jews seem destined to lament.
At last you realized that you
knew nothing more than anybody
knew since there was nothing more
to know.
              Today you settle
for the nails.
                    Meanwhile, the nude
world waits for you to make
a bride of it.
                    Your paintings
prove that nothing's right beyond
perfecting what began with God.
And nothing's left but dancing
on the deathbed of the world
that's always yours for the discovering.
Surviving like the pawn who saved
his queen, you tell the final
bollixer to keep his question marks.
What says you're mortal?
                              Death.
What lets you be immortal?
                              Death.

9. ALL COLORS END IN BLACK

Once you were an actor.
Under the fake whiskers
      and the powdered hair, the man
      inside of you resented being lost
      in character.
                  You faced new roles
      the way a man confronts
      the books he owns but hasn't
      read.
            Finally, you quit.
The audience was always *they*
      and never *you*, the roles
      demanded too much dying
      to yourself, and everything depended
      on applause.
                  You saw your fate
      determined by a boo.
                              Still,
      performing schooled you to the value
      of the hint.
                  The unsaid word
      was louder than a scream, the unmade
      gesture could suggest an avalanche,
      and tears held back were tears
      that no one could ignore.
                              That taught
      you to avoid primary colors
      on your canvases.
                        After the first
      dazzle, what's redder than red?
Even today you let your paler
      colors brighten as the watcher
      watches.
                  Pistachio intensifies

to peppergreen, apple to blood,
lemon to butter, et cetera.
                                Instead
of vomiting a rainbow, you underpaint
the necessary accident.
                                Your *Horse*
in a Billiard Parlor shows
the horse more *horse*, the billiards
more intensely *billiards*.
                                Your oil
of Tipasa makes the sky burst
white above an inch of desert.
One tree is all that punctuates
    the sand the way a navel tightens
    in and down the nakedness around it.
Somehow the whole savannah
    pivots on the peak of one small
    tree that has no reason to be there.
Or once you sketched a nude
    dressed only in a cap until
    the cap was all that anybody saw.
That kind of miracle is all
    you keep between yourself and history.
History says a painter's how
    he lived.
                                And history is right.
Art says a painter's what
    he leaves.
                                And art is right.
The miracle becomes a curse.
As long as all you yield
    to midnight is your shadow, you
    defy the curse by seeing
    what is always there and saying
    so in colors.

Only the dark
can stop you.
                    Or yourself . . .
If you give up, the dark's
    already come.
                    Lately, when you
    sleep, you let the lights
    stay bright.
                    That way
    the scale of colors hums alive
    for you all day, all night.

10. UNDERSTAND THE HIGHWAY, UNDERSTAND
    THE COUNTRY

Driving relaxes you.
                    You like
    the solitude of long trips
    to nowhere in particular.
                    Next
    year you plan to drive due
    north until the last road
    stops in tundra—or south
    as far as Tierra del Fuego.
Why?
            So you can meditate in motion.
Steering down a road, you
    study how the windshield
    frames what's coming
    while the rearview mirror
    telescopes what's gone.
                    The side
    windows smear with presences

83

you can't make out until
they're past.
                          You move against
the earth's swivel.
                     Later, you
sweat to put that feeling into paints
so that your pictures move—
move while you look at them.
No wonder you're at odds with poets.
In your beginning was the picture,
      not the word.
                     Cave paintings,
hieroglyphics—you see them all
as stories for the eye.
                          Television,
film, cartoons?
                     Updated
hieroglyphics, nothing more . . .
For you, the caravan of mile
      after mile never lies
      and never stays the same.
Driving anywhere, you're just
      a speeding witness to God's
      fresco, frame by frame: a boy
      walking a wall as if it were
      a tightrope over hell; two roofers
      shouldering a beam; an overturned
      Buick, its tires spinning
      to a dead roulette.
                          You let them
memorize themselves like postcards
as you go.
                     Maybe you will
read them, maybe not . . .
                               Highwaying,

you look ahead, abreast,
behind like some twinfaced
divinity who sees in retrospect
what's coming while the past
just happens.
                    Or are you King
Ulysses resurrected to repeat
a trek between the world's
absurdities and one man's
luck?
            As long as driving makes
you finally a maker of horizons,
you survive like Cain in Babylon.
The heatwave in the distance
      bends and dances in the wind
      while you roll down the windows,
      slug your will and skill behind
      the wheel, and steer into the chances.

II.   THE NEXT TIME YOU WERE THERE

After Paris, every city's just
      another town.
                        Elephants could roam
      the Metro, Marly's horses
      could invade the Tuileries, wishbone
      arches on the Seine could shatter
      under traffic, and Parisians could
      refuse to estivate in August . . .
Appearing everyday in Paris
      would be Haussmann's Paris, still.
Abroad, you'd like to die the way
      you live in Paris, telescoping four

days into three, believing that your best
is just ahead, protesting
that you need more time, more time,
protesting to the end.
                              And past
the end . . .
                      But you exaggerate.
This capital you share with France
    is just another web—somewhere
    to breathe and board and be.
You bring there what you are,
    and what you are is nowhere
    any different.
                      This makes
    the Trocadero just a penny's patch
    of grass, the Place de la Concorde
    a wide and spindled planisphere,
    and St. Germain-des-Prés another
    church.
                      Weathering your dreams,
    bronze Paris of the doorknobs
    turns into the turning stage
    called *here* that stays the same
    as everywhere right now.
                                    On that
    quick stage a man keeps happening.
From Paris to Paris to Paris,
    the only life he knows
    is anywhere and always coming
    true . . .
                      His name is *you*.

IN THE ORDER OF DISAPPEARANCE

This blue is where the bull shark
    hunts.
           You listen to the smell
of seafall, touch what drowning
means, and taste the thud
of salty alleluias on the beach.
A fish-rib comb proclaims
    that all distinctions fade
    in the diminishing.
               Spar and seawood
rhyme like skeleton with skeleton.
An audience of one, you fish
    the air for sounds, for differences.
For differences?
           They're of the land
    where everything from flint to rosewood
    steadies on the stopped psalms
    of Moses.
           Only the namers change,
    bequeathing to the last minorities
    their sounded pictures, pictured
    songs, and other echoes of the not
    yet thinkable.
           Their carvings chant.
Their songs remind you that forever's
    when it's always now.
           Their gospels
say they primed for death
by trying to imagine how they'd look
asleep.
           Unnameable, they've disappeared
with cavemen, gypsies, sellers
of insurance, saviors, kids,
and numbered kings with all
their bastardies.

They seem to you
like swords honed down, honed
down until there's nothing left
to hone, like grenadella branches
offered to a blaze, like rocks
erased by sledging waterdrops
repeated and repeated.
                    Married
to the moon, this womb of blue
and bone encircles you like zero's
tomb.
            It tells you that by knowing
what you're not, you come
to what you are, and what
you are is just a comma
to the waves.
                    You wait for promises
to prove that you were here.
Undisappearing yet, you wage
yourself against the noosing war
of water and its whirlpool kill.
The script is in the sand.
                        Your toemarks
say the tide scrolls out and in,
the waves keep hilling, milling,
chilling, and the whirlpools win.

CASTAWAY

Purple, navy, aquamarine,
    and emerald, the combers tumble
    brown to Byblos and its walls.
Each wave shatters in blustery
    applause across the reefs, then surfs
    the shallows like a sprinter lunging
    for a tape and pitching through it.
Wave on wave reshuffles, cuts,
    and deals the shore its solitaire
    of shells, leafmuck, or seavines
    webbed around a fin.
                    Blink,
    and everything's sucked back to sea
    again or pummeled undersand.
A tanker on the skyline nudges
    eastward like a target on a rifle
    range.
             Inch by inch its reasons
    tow it out of sight.
                  Or was it
    ever there?
            The sea keeps dealing.

BETWEEN WARS

After the twelve-day storm, the ocean
    settles like a sheet tugged taut.
Instead of being something
    to survive, the dawn is simply
    one more dawn.
                  You lollygag
on deck, deal poker in the hold,
    and shave the beard you now find
    time to shave.
                The mate remembers
    that his ulcer ought to bother him.
Bo's'ns hate their officers again,
    and stokers use the same quick
    nouns to damn the food that they
    had used to pray the winds away.
By noon you wish those weathers
    back when you were just afraid
    to be afraid, when every watch
    meant death or breath, when nothing
    but the storm was real.
                You brag
    that it takes storms to make the sea
    the sea, and sailors sailors.
By night you dream the opposite.
You merely lack the seamanship
    to cope with peaceful waters.

SALTPULSE

When waves attack the sandy
    capes of all the continents
    like young white bulls at dawn
    and old black bulls at dusk,
    you can't pretend they're raging
    for the deaf or charging at the blind.
Rush by rise by rush
    they gallop in until you gallop
    with them.
                Landlocked or rocketing,
    you're of the sea that stays
    three-fourths of everything.
                    Your blood,
    your spittle, and your sweat all
    taste of it.
            It mints the mock
    brine of your son's tears.
It salts the kisses that you give
    your wife.
           At sea your sex
    and seed remember it.
               Ashore
    in space, you watch the turning
    sands go all at once awash
    and settle darkly as a sub
    submerging.
           Hemispheres dissolve.
Uplands become lowlands,
    and lowlands sink until the Baltic
    and the Caribbean touch.
              Then peaks
    and poles go under, and the whole
    sealevel planet dwindles
    to a glint in the swing of a ring
    of the kings of all Calders
    floating in the fathoms of the sun.

REGARDLESS

In this clear sea the drowned
    are who they were again.
Under the night's chalk sun
    they walk the waves like Jesuses
    and chant they'll never die
    until you die.
                They lead you,
    lead you farther, lead you farther
    seaward every moon . . .
                    But this is
Sunday, and the island named Regardless
    offers you its green.
                The wild
pig keeps to the hills.
                Pineapple
and pimento spice the breezes
while you salt and sizzle lamblegs
over charcoals on the beach.
                By dawn
you dance the sailor's dance of
Rhodes, Ukrainian circles,
and the jumps and leaps of Muscovy.
The embers throb like orange hearts,
    burn slowly gray and crumble.
Wading east, you fling
    the lamb bones out to sea
    and sing the morning's yellow moon
    by thirds above the oceanline
    until it bobs the whole way
    up to keep the drowned at bay.

TO DIVE

The bed you ride on rides
   the deck that rides the waves.
Porthole breezes cool your pillow.
Ice water in a pitcher tilts
   to the cabin's pitch, roll,
   and yaw.
               Above you on the dance
floor, an orchestra completes
its sambas.
               Stomping down the hall
in shower clogs, a boy whistles
the Cuban national anthem
flat until his mother quiets
him in Arabic.
              Then, midnight.
Coffee, peppercorns, and copra
   ripen in the hold.
             Brine
swills where the ship's halves
fuse into the keel, and underneath
the keel a manta plunges
like a bomber's shadow through
a clout of smelt.
             Floating
on your sheeted raft, you dream
a dive through halls and holds
and hulls . . .
             You surface breathless
to the naked bride you've loved
a thousand times before.
             Icily,
your bedside pitcher glimmers
amber with the fire of your skins.
Already you are gripping, grappling
   for the first time, again.

KING NOTHING

"Black dog" was Churchill's
    phrase for what I'm facing
    here.
        I keep reporting
    to my desk, my pen, my books,
    but nothing comes of it.
I'm spared confirming Montesquieu's
    "A man can play the fool
    in everything but poetry."
I'm out of poetry right now.
Seamus would shrug and say,
    "When you have nothing to write,
    write nothing."
                Better than
    writing badly.
                Better than fraud.
On T-shirts, matchbooks, and bumper
    stickers, fraud has risen
    to final solutions.
                "Send
    a Cuban home for Christmas!"
"Sickle-cell anemia's
    the great white hope!"
"Arabs can go and reproduce
    themselves!"
            The isms
    in the words explode like spittle
    in my face . . .
            If all we do
    begins in our imagining, I should
    expect the worst more often than
    the best.
            It sells.
                It meets the needs
    of hate.

It happens on command.
It lacks the lightning of the best,
    which comes when it comes to write
    the man the way a dance
    will dance the dancers when the dance
    is right.
        Like love it lets
    the eyes become the face's
    sky again and takes us where
    it takes us—never soon
    enough but not too late.
As long as that's worth
    waiting for, I'll wait.

IN CONVOY

Highways from here, a skunk,
    run over at the neck, stares on.
Like quartz in coal, its eyes
    still multiply all headlights
    and the moon by two.
                        Pastures away,
a rabbit nibbles peach leaves,
and a single daisy times a million
on a mountain shows the stars
what daisypower means.
                        Your
neighborhood's a clutch of prairie
schooners sailing straight
through midnight and beyond.
                        Each
attic whispers by without
an SOS.
         The semaphore of streetlamp
after streetlamp punctuates and codes
the dark.
         Antares flashes pintip-
red above a television aerial.
Seatight inside your shiphouse,
    you have no port except to stay
    afloat as long as possible.
                  On watch,
you puff your briar and inscribe
ink entries in a log.
                Your pen's
your mightier sword.
                Its drawn point
duels the mute riot of everything.

Too busy saying what you choose,
    your words rush straight ahead
    like some unsteady solo
    in the key of reason.
                    No sharps,
no flats, nothing left to syncopation,
not a hint of dazzle.
                    Predictably,
the final words that end
the final lines must kiss—
like this.
            Dominoes!
                    The world
keeps waiting for a voice to tell
it what it means while you
play dominoes.
                    Even your days
are dominoes.
                    You count your steps.
Each dawn you brush your up-teeth
    down and then your down-teeth
    up.
        The spaced and slowly
    sinking heartbeat of a deathbell
    sobers every ear but yours.
Remember Ivan's words on death?
"The dead outnumber us—we all
    must join that last majority—
    to die is simply democratic."
Could you have uttered that
    and slapped your knee and laughed?
Remember too the girl you quietly
    desired and thought you loved
    but never made love to?
                    Facing

the possibility of pleasure
and the certainty of guilt, you
backed into the future like a thief.
At worst you're still a puritan,
    still ready to retreat into a simpler
    world that's always waiting to receive
    the man you think you are.
At best you live by Goethe's creed
    that thought begins in private,
    character in public.
              Alone
    with dreams you can't refute
    and wants you never want to want,
    you turn to words until
    you turn into the words you write.
Your metronome collapses, and your
    lines unrhyme while you go on
    committing poetry, that holy crime.

FLYING DOWN THE DREAM

It's like tobogganing.
                    You scud
      the frosted cupolas of clouds
      instead of snow, thumping
      over bumps of turbulence
      but otherwise at peace.
                    Tan
      coffee seesaws in your plexicup.
Across the aisle three sailors
      argue over five-card stud.
Beside you in the windowseat,
      a fourth unfolds by thirds
      a centerpage of pelvis, breasts,
      and then the rest of Miss July . . .
Five minutes west of home, you try
      imagining what's going on below.
Your son should be in school.
Your wife might be addressing
      envelopes.
                    Aging apart from them,
      you're like Ulysses viewing Ithaca
      from heaven . . .
                    Thunderstatic
      shakes the fuselage like flak,
      and down you drop.
                    Buzzers buzz,
      and seatbelt signs blink red
      in lower-case American and French.
Spilt, your coffee tans
      the sunspared ass of Miss July.
The galley's hardware rattles
      like a carnival of cans behind
      a wedding car.
                    You tell yourself
      what's happening's not happening.

You bless and hold your holy
    breath.
            Everyone aboard
    becomes your brother and your sister
    all at once.
                You think about
    your wife and son without you . . .
Swallowing the choking from your ears,
    you watch the cabin lensing
    back to focus, caliber by caliber.
A stewardess appears, all smiles
    and amnesia.
                Over the intercom
    the captain's "really sorry about that."
The sailor at your elbow shakes
    your coffee from his page and pages
    back before he pages on.
                        And you?
You wait until the steadily ascending
    planet turns into the underrolling
    runway at the ending . . .
                    And you breathe.

THE BEARING

Heavy from her steady bellying,
    the mare comes due.
                  No memory
    of ten Kentuckies or the horse farms
    east of Buffalo prepares you
    for the silk of that first fur.
You've seen the Easter foals stilting
    in toy gallops by their almost
    inattentive mothers.
                  You've known
    from watching what the breeding
    of Arabia will hone from all
    that spindliness: in weeks, the fetlocks
    shapelier; in months, the girth below
    the withers sinewed like a harp;
    in years, the stance and prancing
    that will stop a crowd.
But now the colt's nose nudging
    for horsemilk nullifies a dream
    to come of stallions.
                  Now
    it is enough to know that something
    can arrive so perfectly and stand
    upright among so many fallen
    miracles and, standing, fill
    the suddenly all-sacred barn
    with trumpets and a memory of kings.

A CITY MADE SACRED BECAUSE YOUR SON'S GRANDFATHER DIED IN IT

Your father in a wheelchair slouches
   steeply to his stroked-out side.
Your son wheels for the final
   time his final grandfather.
And you, who've walked this street
   so many times you know
   the slope and crack of every
   sidewalk square, just walk
   behind.
            You ask your son
   (or is it just your son?)
   to slow things down.
Your father flicks his good
   right hand to say he can't
   accept but won't deny what's
   happened, that not accepting
   what is unacceptable is all
   life meant or means to him.
You want to hold his other
   hand and squeeze it back
   to life until the doctors
   and their facts relent.
            The doctors
   and their facts go on.
            So do
   the unaffected riders in the numbered
   buses.
          So does the whole
   damn city that becomes no more
   than just a place to live
   and die in now.
            The more you walk,
   the less you know the street
   you knew.

The less you know,
the more the curbs become
opposing shores.
                    The street
is suddenly the river no man
steps in twice or finally outswims.
Midway between your father
and your son, you feel yourself
drawn in and on and under.

THE DAY YOUR SON WAS BORN, IT IS

Last night you saw it hooded,
    silent, sipping from the saucer
    of a child's skull a child's
    blood.
           Tonight it puts aside
    that holy wine and leaves you
    falling like a dreamer in a void.
It is the darker twin of love.
It comes when you are least
    or most prepared.
              It is the viper
    in your sock, the sand that bogs
    you to a stop, the scream
    you strain to scream but never
    scream.
          Awake, you ask
    the night if what you dream
    is what all fathers dream.
Your midnight house keeps talking
    to itself.
           A nightlight paints
    a gargoyle on the ceiling while
    you smoke another inch from yesterday's
    cigar.
          For minutes you mistake it
    in the smoke until you recognize
    the hood, the face averted
    and the rest in shadow.
              Silent,
    it stays as near as air.
              It bids
    at baccarat with something in another
    hood.
          Call that its mirror trick.
Call that its solitaire for two

or give it any name that shows
how fear and fear's illusions
are the same.
            As long as you
go on, so does the game.

THE DUEL THAT IS VERTICAL

Nearing the world of nine
    Novembers, he astounds you,
    makes you dream of reruns,
    maddens you for missing what
    can only happen once or never.
Cheek against your arm, he asks
    you how we hear—exactly how?
You talk of waves, vibrations,
    tympany and then give up.
Lately you give up on more
    and more—on God, on death,
    on whether goldfish sleep
    or where the sky stops.
                  Before
undoubtful doubts, you stand
on ignorance.
               You stall the vaccination
of the facts.
            You answer mystery
with mystery.
            Headed as a pair
for sleep, you play a game
that knights you in the name
of wonder.
           Flying buses
stand for jets—freighters
are sea-trucks—applause is happy
noise, and so on.
           He leads.
You counter.
        Almost asleep,
he tells you how he dreams
of chasing lions through Alaska
on his bike.
          You ask him

if he's heard there are
no lions in Alaska.
                    He says
there are if he can dream there are.
Before undreamers undeceive him,
    you believe him, dream by dream.

NIGHT LETTER TO AMERICA ON
SWITZERLAND'S INDEPENDENCE DAY

What Calvin called the body
 of this death is memory enough
 for you.
    Which memory?
        If you
remembered that, you'd prophesy
just how you'll die.
      Ignorant,
you face your term and time
the way a pregnant woman
faces labor, certain of the *if*
but doubtful of the *how* and *when*
and always of the *why*.
       Bearing
with a different *why,* you labor on.
No fate prefigures yours, not Rilke
 in Muzot, not Henry of the last
 addresses, not bombed commandos
 trucked like carcass beef
 from skirmishes, not Charles de Gaulle
 at solitaire (at solitaire!) convulsed
 and taken.
     Anticipating or remembering,
you're left with words.
       Assured
that what you write will matter
more in Europe than in all
the States, you see your country
flawed with hollows.
      Half
its citizens have never learned
its creeds.
    What's left of Jefferson's
once "solid . . . independent yeomanry"
is paid to grow, then burn

its crops.
                Good lakes and better
clouds are fouled with the filth
of mills, and men whose clothes
are costumes bark the day's bad
news as if their mouths were anuses . . .
Beneath Geneva's current carnival
    of seven centuries of fireworks,
    you see the light.
                        Americans are not
America—not yet.
                    The dynamo
of Henry Adams pulses like a tumor
in their skulls.
                        The motor runs and runs.
Dying's a stoppage; love,
    a diversion; sickness, a delay;
    children, an inconvenience.
What's left?
                If happiness is not
the same as freedom, love,
children, and the art of work,
what is it?
                The Swiss respond
by being Swiss as certainly
as all their clocks repeat themselves
two times a day.
                    You wish
your countrymen that much
of someone else's history.
                        You say
so in this pilgrim's telegram
and post it to be opened in event
of death.
                You never mention whose.

ONLY THE NEW BRANCHES BLOOM

For Grace, 7/19/78

Denying what it means to doubt,
   this year's forsythias unfold
   and flood the air with yellow
   answers.
               They say it's time
   I opened up, time I learned
   French, time I liked less
   and loved more, time
   I listened to the sun, time
   I made time.
                 Why not?
Can days of making sense
   of days that make no sense
   make sense?
               If nothing's sure
   but nothing's sure, then reading
   Montesquieu must wait.
Preparing for my enemies must
   wait.
           And gravity the hurrier
   must wait because forsythias
   are happening.
               They make me
   turn my back on facts,
   insurance policies, inoculations,
   wire barbed or braided,
   bodyguards, and all the folderol
   of fear.
            They say that this
   year's blossoms will outlive
   the lasting death of Mars.
There are no flowers on the stars.

LEAFING

Bagged and burned, they turn
    into the only smoke that's worth
    the tasting.
                Woods revert
    to wood as I, their janitor,
    rake up the year.
                  Cleansed,
    cleansed to my tree of bones
    and savoring the blown tobacco
    of November, I recall Chateaubriand's
    "Forests precede civilizations,
    and deserts follow them."
Disturbing comments for a ballpoint
    era where psychiatry's the state
    religion, and the prize of prizes
    is a champagne shampoo
    in the locker room.
                My woods
    are far from forests, but I know
    real deserts when I see them.
So, I work my bonewood rake,
    leafing for reasons to repudiate
    Chateaubriand.
                The answer's
    in the trees.
                Shorn to their shells,
    they'll wait the winter out
    and start all over when
    the time is right.
                By then
    the desert's prize and predecessors
    will have gone the way of smoke.
As long as there's a leaf, there's hope.

THE TOYS

Wing to wing, they bake
  in weather that can sizzle bacon
  on their stars.
                        Fighters, bombers,
  trainers—Arizona stores them all
  unrusting in a prophecy of yesterday.
West by half the Pacific, the holy
  salvage of another *Arizona*
  consecrates Pearl Harbor like a church . . .
If wreckages were pages, nothing
  could book them.
                        Cain's garbage
  mines the Baltic, fouls
  forty years of bracken near
  Cassino, spoils Guam's lagoon.
What were these havocs to their crews
  but new toys for an old game?
As facts left over from a fact,
  they speak for history ahead
  of all that history remembers
  to predict about the tactics of our kind.
Cain's rock and rocket
  leave us nothing new to find.
In North America the oldest skull's
  a woman's, brained from behind.

LONG DISTANCE ISN'T

Separated by a sea, two shores,
    the clans of Vercingetorix, the Brenner
    Pass, the boot of Italy
    from just below the knee to halfway
    down the calf, we nix them all
    by phone.
                Our voices kiss.
Who cares if the Atlantic bashes
    Maine, Land's End, or Normandy?
We leapfrog hemispheres the way
    the mind cavorts through God-knows-what
    millennia, what dynasties, what
    samples of our kind from
    australopithecus to Charlie Chaplin.
The body's place?
                Cross latitude
    by longitude, and it is there.
The body's age?
              Count up
    from birth or back from death,
    and it is there.
              But words?
We launch them out like vows
    against the wind.
                Creating what we are,
    they wing through seas and continents
    and make us more than elegies
    to yesterday.
              Forget the cost.
Talk louder and ignore the static.
Pretend we're walking through the dark.
Don't stop.
           Don't stop or look
    behind you.
           As long as you
    keep talking, I can find you.

DUBLIN TWILIGHT

From Parnell's statue to O'Connell's
    I can smell America's sixties
    when the center did not hold.
Priests resemble priests, and nuns
    are nuns.
                    A Shaw play runs
    at the Abbey.
                        Arrayed in rows
    beside the *Summa Theologica,*
Joyce sells well while his bones
    age in Zurich.
                        "No nation
    has the right to fix the boundary
    to the march of a nation," wrote Parnell
    before the troubles and the tans.
Locked in this city of drizzle,
    soot, and kindness, the only
    march is traffic and shoppers.
Alighting on O'Connell's granite
    scalp, a pigeon perches
    like some dirty dove of hope.
It stares and stays while Yeats'
    lion-bodied saviors battle
    in Belfast, and a Liffey sidewalk
    slogan damns the pope.

THE SILENCE AT THE BOTTOM OF THE WELL

It's been expecting me so long
    that I feel late.
                Dropped
stones are what it's thirsty for,
and I've come armed . . .
                      I hear
the ghosts of splashes plummet
upward like the tired swallows
of a heart near death.
                   If I
could dunk and hoist a bucket,
I would taste what mountain
brooks remember of the snow.
Instead, I whisper down
    my name, my name, my name
    and listen as it yoyos
    in a rounding echo back,
    back, back . . .
                Below the parapet
the swirling walls dive
farther down than I can dream.
Deeper, where night and water
    meet, the moon of the assassins
    waits for yesterday, and never sleeps.

THE TIME IT IS IN SOFIA

No whistles now, no horns . . .
A thousand moons float flat
   on rain lakes, bobbing
    as the wind bends over them.
Birdchant and dogtalk wrangle
   in the almost dawn.
               They surface
  all at once like lights
  that blink awake on dark oceans.
I squint for them as I
   might listen to my pulse
   or to a woman humming naked
   in another room.
           The only
  other sentries are the stars . . .
What is it to the stars if I
   imagine watchmen somewhere
   chewing silent bread
   and silent cheese, a farmer
   somewhere silencing a stallion,
   lovers somewhere sleeping off
   the sweet pain that ends
   in ecstasy?
          My dreams rain
  down into the holy wisdom
  of the facts.
         Beyond the Russian
Embassy, a pair of soccer
players walk a soccer
ball between them as they sing.
The stars are light enough
   to see them home with still
   the taste of victory and vodka
   in their eyes.
         They disappear

but stay the way skywriting
disappears but stays forever
in the mind's sure sky.
                              For years
I'll hear them clapping in Bulgarian.

I say what Lindbergh's father
    said to Lindbergh: "One boy's
    a boy; two boys are half
    a boy; three boys are no
    boy at all."
            Which helps explain
    why Lindbergh kept his boyishness
    for life, which meant he stayed
    himself, which means a lot.
What else is destiny?
            After
    you learn that governments lie
    and happiness is undefinable
    and death has no patience,
    you'll understand me.
            Meanwhile,
    the ignorant but well informed
    will try to keep you mute
    as a shut book.
            Forecasters of the best
    and worst will hurry to retreat
    infallibly into the future.
            Ministers
    who talk on cue with God
    will weigh you down like serious
    furniture.
            Assume that what
    you lose to such distractions
    you will gain in strength.
By then you'll learn that all
    you know will help you less
    than how you think.
            The rest
    is memory, and memory's the graveyard
    of the mind as surely as tomorrow

is its myth.
                    Nowhere but the time
at hand is when you'll see
that God's geometry is feast
enough.
                    Within the world's
closed circles, everything's
the sum of halves that rhyme.
From coconuts to butterflies
    to lovers knotted on the soft
    battlefield of any bed, the halves
    add up to one, and every
    one remembers where it came
    from as a trumpet note
    recalls the song it was a part of
    and the listeners who heard it
    and were changed.
                    What Lindbergh's
father meant and what I mean
are two roads to the same
country.
            Knowing how long
it takes us to be young, he left
his son some clues to get
his bearings by.
                    And so do I.

SILENCE SPOKEN HERE

What absence only can create
   needs absence to create it.
Split by deaths or distances,
   we all survive like exiles
   from the time at hand, living
   where love leads us for love's
   reasons.
           We tell ourselves
   that life, if anywhere, is there.
Why isn't it?
           What keeps us
   hostages to elsewhere?
             The dead
   possess us when they choose.
The far stay nearer than we know
   they are.
           We taste the way
   they talk, remember everything
   they've yet to tell us, dream
   them home and young again
   from countries they will never leave.
With friends it's worse and better.
Together, we regret the times
   we were apart.
           Apart, we're
   more together than we are
   together.
           We say that losing
   those we love to living
   is the price of loving.
            We say
   such honest lies because
   we must—because we have
   no choices.
           Face to face
   we say them, but our eyes
   have different voices.

I'm tired of living for tomorrow's
    headlines, tired of explanations,
    tired of letters that begin "Dear
    patriot . . ." or else "You may
    already be the winner of . . ."
I'm near the point where nothing's
    worth the time.
                The causes
    I believe in rarely win.
The men and women I admire
    most are quietly ignored.
What's called "the infinite
    progression of the negative" assumes
    if I can count to minus seven,
    I can count to seven
    million, which means the bad
    can certainly be worse, and that
    the worse can certainly, et cetera . . .
Regardless, I believe
    that something in me always was
    and will be what I am.
I make each day my revolution.
Each revolution is a wheel's full
    turn where nothing seems the same
    while everything's no different.
I want to shout in every dialect
    of silence that the world we dream
    is what the world becomes,
    and what the world's become
    is there for anyone's re-dreaming.
Even the vanishing of facts
    demands a consecration: the uncolor
    of champagne, the way that presidential
    signatures remind me of a heartbeat's
    dying scrawl across a monitor,

the languages that earlobes speak
when centered by enunciating pearls,
the sculpture of a limply belted
dress, the instant of bite
when grapes taste grape.
                              The range
of plus is no less infinite
than minus . . .
                              I learn that going
on means coming back
and looking hard at just one thing.
That rosebush, for example.
A single rose on that bush.
The whiteness of that rose.
                              A petal
of that whiteness.
                              The tip
of that petal.
                              The curl of that tip.
And just like that the rose
in all its whiteness blooms
within me like a dream so true
that I can taste it.
                              And I do.

THE QUIET PROOFS OF LOVE

When your son has grown up, treat him like
your brother.
                                    —ARAB PROVERB

Don't wait for definitions.
                              I've had
      my fill of aftertalk
      and overtalk, of meanings that don't
      mean, of words not true
      enough to be invisible, of all
      those Januaries of the mind when
      everything that happens happens
      from the eyebrows up.
                              If truth
      is in the taste and not
      the telling, give me whatever
      is and cannot be again—
      like sherbet on the tongue, like love . . .
Paris defined is Paris
      lost, but Paris loved
      is always Orly in the rain,
      broiled pork and chestnuts
      near the Rue de Seine,
      the motorcade that sped de Gaulle
      himself through Montparnasse.
                                    Viva

      the fool who said, "Show me
      a man who thinks, I'll show
      you a man who frowns."
                              Which
      reminds me of Andrew, learning
      to count by twos and asking,
      "Where is the end of counting?"
Let's settle for the salt and pepper
      of the facts.
                        Oranges don't parse,

and no philosopher can translate
shoulders in defeat or how
it feels when luck's slim arrow
stops at you or why lovemaking's
not itself until it's made.
Let's breathe like fishermen who sit
alone together on a dock
and let the wind do all
the talking.
                    That way we'll see
that who we are is what
we'll be hereafter.
                    We'll learn
the bravery of trees that cannot
know "the dice of God
are always loaded."
                    We'll think
of life as one long kiss
since talk and kisses never mix.
We'll watch the architecture
of the clouds create themselves
like flames and disappear like laughter.

SONG FOR THE FLIES OF FIRE

The fifty-year-old girl of twenty
    said, "In love it's best
    to be cynical."
                    She'd modeled, acted
    in French commercials, and sung
    rock with a group called
    "Soviet Sex."
                    Her eyes were cat's
    eyes but without the mystery.
Her smile faded like tired foam
    or like a memory of Berryman,
    who, when all he spoke and wrote
    was poetry, decided he was through.
That's how it ends with some.
Burn fast, burn out . . .
                    Even
    the repenters live clichés
    that guarantee oblivion.
                    Grundy,
    who put himself through college
    selling marijuana, prosecutes
    for Justice now in Washington.
Eldridge Cleaver shouts
    like Billy Sunday.
                    Nixon's
    cronies milk the lecture
    circuit, publish fiction,
    and believe with all their re-born
    might in President Jesus . . .
I think like this while watching
    lightning bugs play midnight
    tag around my house.
                    Ignite
    and pause.
                    Ignite and pause—

each one its own Prometheus,
a sun in flight, a type
of Edison.
                    They burn like signals
hyphenated by the breath of night.
Each time I think they're burning out
    instead of on, they burn again
    like pulses that will just not die.
Their brightness lightens me.
It's no small thing to bear
    a dawn within you.
                    It's
even more at midnight to create
with nothing but your being
plus a light that tunes the darkness
something like the music of the sky.

UNTO THE ISLANDS

Each dawn I slew the sand
   behind Grand Case toward
   the cape where Jackie O
   is building her alternative.
                        Upbeach,
   two naked mermaids snorkel
   through the surf, their backs
   awash with ocean suds, their gleaming
   bottoms, like O'Murphy's, dolphining
   in tandem as their finned feet
   churn.
           A poem I've been planning
   pulls apart.
             The more I mine
   for nouns and fish for verbs
   the more it pulls apart.
                 By noon
   the almost breathing sea assumes
   the fully female languor
   of a woman sleeping naked
   on a beach—her breasts re-shaping
   as she turns, her thighs dividing
   like abandonment itself, her mating
   slot so free of shame it shows
   its secret to the sun.
              I tell
   myself I'm here like Jackie O,
   and for a week it's true.
               The time
   is always sun o'clock, and every
   day is Sunday.
           The nights
   are stars and coffee and a netted
   bed.
       But all around me live
   black men with Dutch and French
   and Spanish names and blood

so mixed that all the scars
of slavery bleed through.
                              Daily
they show me history in sepia.
That history's defunct and all
the slavers sunk, but still
the only church is Catholic Dutch.
The menus mimic Europe,
and a drunk whose middle name
is Van distributes all the Heinekens
in town.
                    But who am I
to criticize?
                    An ex-colonial myself,
I can't distinguish custom
in my life from conscience, and I
end half-Calvinist half-hedonist
with nothing to confess but
contradiction.
                    Island or mainland,
what's the difference?
                              Until
a poem I cannot deny denudes
me into life, I'm just another
pilgrim passing through the obvious.
I need a true alternative
when now is never long
enough to write down what
I know.
                    Instead I stay a tan
away from who I was a hemisphere
ago.
          I'm western history
revisited.
                    I'm souvenirs and sun
revisited.
                    I pay my way and go.

CLEAN BREAK

My ankle broke me when it broke
    and made me tell a different
    kind of time.
                    Baths were projects,
    stairs precipitous up or down,
    and crutches like the wings of penguins,
    second-rate but indispensable.
Asked, I told what happened
    with embellishments: the fall,
    the treatment in emergency, the splint,
    the X-rays, and the nurse's question
    just before the spinal and the surgery,
    "Which ankle are we fixing
    anyway?"
                A friend informed me
    that a skater cracked her leg
    my way, was splinted to the crotch,
    and ended pregnant while recovering.
"Where there's a will, there's
    a way," she hummed.
                    "Where
    there's a way, there's a will,"
    I countered, pondering positions
    and the artistry in question.
                      Once
    home, I read *Ulysses*, grouted
    tiles, and revered anew
    the names of Alexander Graham Bell
    and Thomas Edison and Clarence
    Fax, who housed our stereo
    accessibly.
                I re-evaluated friends
    and loved the good ones more,
    the better more so, and the best
    ones most.
                So many flowers
    came I thought I died

until I realized death-flowers
molder with the dead while mine
bloomed on at home.
                              Harvey's card
was in-house made, but Mickey's
offered free the surest cure:
"Four parts gin, one part
vermouth, serve with olive,
repeat dosage until this recipe
becomes difficult to read."
Dr. Ward was not amused.
Having added three titanium
    screws to both my chemistry
    and weight, he counseled patience,
    caution, and intelligent restraint.
I practiced these with moderate
    success until a telephoning
    priest reminded me, "Respect
    your doctor, or I'll kick your ass."
Thereafter, I obeyed.
                              Having
    watched collegians ride
    their crutches through the wind
    like skiers' poles, I vowed
    to stay advisedly incompetent.
That way if Mary Burnham
    cautioned me again to break
    a leg before I went on stage,
    I'd wink and say I did
    and wore a cast from Valentine's
    to Good Friday, conveniently
    parenthesizing love and death.
Then I'd tell her how
    I rose in both my socks
    in both my shoes and walked
    like Jesus on the water back
    to everything I did so easily
    before that easy memory went crack.

THE CLOAK OF FORTUNATUS

For Edward Mattos

You left too soon so suddenly,
   and all your skill and wit
   and generous skulduggery went
   with you like a fire fading
   into smoke and back to air . . .
                          Just now
   your letter, written on your last
   live day, arrived.
                It took
   the vengeance from your exit
   since you talked about "the next
   roller coaster ride" and thanked me
   for my thanks.
             "This, happily,
   seems to be my lot," you said
   with just the right degree
   of poise and peppery resilience.
Like any father, artist, or perfectionist
   with more to do than time
   to do it, you did the best
   you could and left the rest
   to God and a martini.
                "The cloak
   of Fortunatus," you resumed, "keeps
   one from being too annoyed
   and too frustrated."
             I checked
   the reference and came up dry
   and now prefer it unexplained.
But still it vexes me the way
   it vexes me to say that no one's
   life concludes as planned.
             There's

always something left undone,
unthought, untold, and we depart
unfinished as the world,
which goes on being what
we tried or failed to make it
while we had the chance.
Like Peter Sarkis, who could still
thank God the same for life
and dying, we can go in gratitude
for what we had.
                Or we can fight
like Helen Middleton, who had
her hand still fisted, even
in the coffin.
                Or we can leave
like you with all sails full.
But still we're missed as you are
missed right now.
                I'm glad
we took the time to make
the most of time.
                I'm proud
we worked where poetry and music
danced and kissed.
                I'm grateful
for the said and unsaid words
and for the sung and unsung songs.
I only wish these lines
had never to be written, Ed.
No matter what they say,
they leave too much unsaid,
and still my hand's a fist.

THE LAST PHOTOGRAPH OF JOHN CIARDI

It shows you at your best address—
    behind a podium and speaking
    poetry aloud, your own and Dante's.
Whoever heard you heard grandmothers
    praying in Italian, echoes
    of Pacific gunnery, the deft
    excoriation of the small of soul
    and how a word can grow
    through seven centuries, three
    languages, and twenty dialects
    into itself.
              Prolific phonies
    bored you.
              Right-angled minds
    from Cambridge bored you more.
Chirpers from Manhattan and the Merritt
    Parkway bored you most.
              You
    left them to the pet awards
    they gave themselves and spoke
    an audience to birth that was
    too good for them . . .
              The language
    called American is less because
    you left it, John, but more
    because of what you left of it
    to us.
        I'm thinking of the poems,
    prose, and conversations that were
    really conversations.
             Once
    we talked MacLeish—his boyhood
    voice, the perfect carpentry of how
    he spoke, his utter lack of cant
    or spite.

I told you that his
final words were to his son:
"You go along."
                    It made you think
of someone somewhere in the *Purgatorio*—
a warrior who died with half
the name of Mary on his lips . . .
But nowhere were you better
    than you were in repartee.
                            Offered
    the *Obituary Journal* by a young
    obituarian, you winked and said
    it should give birth to *Son
    of Obituary Journal.*
                        That brand
    of Ciardi-ness will never die
    as long as I'm alive to quote it . . .
After your death I heard your
    browser's voice on NPR.
"Good words to you," was how
    you closed.
                    Had you had time
    ahead of time to choose last words,
    you might have chosen those
    to be your jauntiest goodbye.

HARPSONG

Its green forepillar glistens
    clean as archery and surges
    forward like a keel.
                No harpist,
I delivered it from junkdom
    for the plain geometry of how
    it curved.
            With scarce a string
    but Gaelic surely to its pins,
    my harp speaks more to me
    of Ireland than its flag.
                I think
of years when none could take
    by law from any Irish man
    his books, his sword, his harp.
I think of Cromwell's soldiers
    smashing first the harps
    in every Irish house
    to crush the spirit of "this rabble
    race."
        Poem or weapon,
    my *cláirseach's* both at once—
    something to pluck in peace,
    in war a prize that Cromwells
    break.
        It treasures in its every
    key the joy of sorrow
    and the grief of ecstasy.
              No wonder
then I house it holy
    as a sword among my books
    for my and even Cromwell's sake.

FLORENCE BY PROXY

October's ochre changes
    everything to Italy.
                            Sunpainted
    walls remember villas
    near Fiesole.
                        I've never seen
    Fiesole.
                    Some day I will,
    and it will seem a memory
    of noon in the United States
    when I became a Florentine
    because the sun bewildered me.
Who among the Florentines
    is listening?
                        Who else but me
    who sees in the Italians
    the human race that Goethe
    saw . . .
                    Today their cops
    are commodores; their Fiats,
    weapons in their whizzing duels
    on the road; their shoes and gloves,
    the very renaissance of calf.
Tribal to the death, they swear
    by their mothers, breastfeed
    their sons wherever, prefer
    their pasta three-fourths cooked,
    and sing whatever whenever . . .
Mistaken for Italian half
    my life, I'm of the tribe.
If it's Italian to speak
    in tears before goodbyes,
    I qualify.
                    If it's Italian
    to choose tomatoes one

by one, I qualify.
                    If it's
Italian to laugh when no one
else is laughing or to whistle
at the wheel, I qualify.
                         One
murmur in Italian soothes
the Florentine in me that French
confuses, German contradicts,
and Spanish misses by a hair.
One murmur, and I feel
    what Goethe felt when Florence
    wounded him with Italy
    for life though Goethe spent
    not quite three hours there.

Her heroines were Pola Negri,
   Gloria Swanson, and Mae West—
   one for glamour, one for style,
   one for nerve.
              First on her scale
of praise came courage of the heart,
then brains, then something called
in Arabic "lightbloodedness."
                    All
   birds but owls she loved, all
   that was green and growable,
   including weeds, all operas
   in Italian, the schmaltzier the better . . .
Lightning she feared, then age
   since people thought the old
   "unnecessary," then living on
   without us, then absolutely nothing.
Each time I'd say some girl
   had perfect legs, she'd tell me
   with a smile, "Marry
   her legs."
              Or if I'd find
a project difficult, she'd say,
"Your mother, Lottie, mastered
Greek in seven months."
Or once when Maris bested Ruth's
   home runs by one, she said,
   "Compared to Ruth, who's Harris?"
Crying while she stitched my shirt,
   she said, "You don't know
   what to suffer is until
   someone you love is suffering
   to death, and what can you do?"
On principle she told one bishop
   what she thought of him.

On personality she called one
   global thinker temporarily
   insane.
            She dealt a serious
   hand of poker, voted
   her last vote for Kennedy,
   and wished us a son two years
   before he came.
            She hoped
   that she would never die
   in bed.
            And never she did.
"When you and your brother were young,"
   she said, "and I was working,
   then was I happy."
            And she was.
The folderol of funerals disgusted
   her enough to say, "I'm
   telling no one when
   I die."
            And she didn't.
One night she jotted down
   in longhand on a filing card,
   "I pray to God that I'll be
   with you always."
            And she is.

MARY ANNE'S ON ANY ANNIVERSARY

Remember Canada?
We pooled
our dollars and we went,
relying only on each other
and a car that had its problems.
Since then our counterpoints
persist.
I hate fast
and love slow while you're
the opposite.
I'm Centigrade.
You're Fahrenheit.
I throw away.
You treasure.
I hear the words
and trace the silhouettes.
You learn
the rhythm and enjoy the colors.
If every day's the picnic
after Adam's dream, we're picnickers.
En route to anywhere, we bicker
as we go but come home
happy.
What bonds us then?
A love of figure-skating,
manners, courage, and the poetry
of being kind?
Or just
that difference makes no
difference to the heart.
Confirmed
by how we faced three deaths
together and a birth that answered
everything, we're sure of nothing
but the going on.

We take
our chances like Freud's "group
of two" whose only books are stars
and waves and what the wind
is doing . . .
                    Queen of the right
word and when it should be
said, I love you for the way
you keep surprising me by being
you.
          Who else could whisper
through the pentothal before
your surgery, "If anything goes
wrong, take care of Sam."
Then to prove the woman in you
    never sleeps, you added, "How
    do I look?"
                    Darling, no wonder
every child and flower opens up
to you.
          You can't be unreceiving
or deceiving if you want to,
and you've yet to want to.
That's your mystery.
                         If "love
plus desperation equals poetry,"
then love plus mystery is all
the desperation I deserve to learn.
On cold nights or warm
    I'll turn and tell you this,
    not loud enough to wake you,
    but in secret, softly, like a kiss.

THE FIRST THIRTIETH

If loving is "the laughter of two
   bodies," we've laughed a lot
   and loved it.
            But every laugh's
   the first for us as every
   breath or day or anniversary's
   the first.
         Who was it said
   that God despises those
   who count?
           Why bother over
   sums if marriage seems
   as briefly long as one full
   day and one short night?
Let all the counters count
   their way to June eleventh
   thirty years ago.
          They'll end
   with history, mere history,
   since all that counting does
   is lock you in the world.
For lovers, one plus one plus
   one add up to times
   when time's irrelevant since love
   has made them one another's time,
   and that's the time that keeps.
They feel the sleep of memory
   become today as quietly
   as all their words and whispers
   turn into the air.
          Flowers
   speak that language.
             And the wind.
And kisses when it makes
   no difference where or why . . .

Over the Atlantic once
    I bought an in-flight watch
    that told and tells time twice—
    this minute and the time it is
    in Paris.
                    Let's call the time
    it is right now in Paris
    something like the time we tell.
Always differently identical,
    it happens orangely in Italy,
    olively in Egypt, orchidly
    in Monaco, crimsonly in Barcelona,
    silverly in London, greenly
    in Kilkenny, balsamly near Saranac,
    and steady as the sun at home.
Even if it ends, we'll laugh
    and say we're still not done
    because we're only just beginning
    what we always have begun.

THROES

I

To learn a woman, to memorize
    the glide of her breasts between
    her blouse's wings, to watch
    her deep in mother-thinking
    just before she sleeps . . .
                    These
are secrecies.
             She hides from you
the fear you've seen in fisherwives
who wait ashore alone
for men who farm or hunt
the sea.
           Tears are her truest
language, and all the dialects
of silence happen in her eyes.
Why should she tatter what
    she feels with talk?
               Facing
her body's face, you see
her be the woman she might be
when showering or swirling
in a waltz of dreams or waking
naked to the naked sun
in Tuscany.
           If you say only
what evades you in the saying,
she will hear you to the end.
Because she knows that love
    means joining loneliness
    to loneliness to make one
    solitude, she seems like one
    remembering the future
    and distrusting it.
               How can she

tell you this?
                    Or why?
                              Or when?

2

Dancing, you forget how
    oakflakes fall and flatten
    like a thousand duckprints
    on October's lawn.
                         You forget
    the poems you will never
    write and everything that came
    to you in dreams and left
    in dreams.
                    You forget the dead
    you'll both become and all
    the dead your loving keeps
    alive.
               Like coupled nouns
    you turn into the dancing verb
    that's born and dies each time
    you dance it.
                    Waist to waist,
    you dance your world between
    you and complete together all
    you lack alone as steady
    frictions make a single fire.
Don't think about the music.
You're the music!
                    Obey
    your feet and dance until
    your dancing proves that dance
    and dancer are the same as love
    and lovers when they meet.

3

In this new land your enemies
 are maps and almanacs
 and anything that counts the time.
Wounded with absence, you
 convalesce apart.
      Each
 memory you made is like
 the Renaissance or the great age
 of sail—unique but unrepeatable.
Alone, you're at the mercy
 of your eyes.
      They never had
 enough.
     They spoke the only
 language you could understand.
Now blind and mute, you learn
 that loneliness and being left
 alone are unalike as twin
 from twin—not much, but enough.
If you explain your frowns
 to anyone but her, you might
 as well be speaking Japanese.
Some days are long held breaths . . .
Is this an exile or the way
 you'll be forever?
      Why can't you
 be like gods who change
 into the wind and back
 to prove no loss is mortal
 but the last?
     Where can you
 go if you possess within
 yourselves each other's

compass and address?
                              Each thought's
a plan.
              Each plan's a loss . . .
You live as best you can.

4

You meet, and there's the sun
    again like God's first light.
Your blind eyes speak.
                              Your
    mute eyes read your
    facing faces.
                  Sooner
    than the sudden rose of your
    first kiss, you solve each
    other with a look as perfectly
    as keys solve locks.
                          You toast
    from the same cup a time
    you're always just remembering
    as never time enough.

5

If you draw back from her,
    you see her nearer, clearer,
    dearer.
              Not what the Nikon
    sees—the wink when she wins,
    the caught curve of her smile,
    the way the least injustice
    cocks the trigger in her jaw.
Instead, you seem to see
    the ache of no one there—

her dresses on their hangers
never to be worn again—
her mirror silent as an empty
stage—her side of the bed
like winter forever.
                              If that's
the risk, what's left but loving
as the last defiance?
                              Ongoing
as your blood, you live
uncornered in your cornered rooms
like paintings space alone
can frame.
                    You let no more
than who you are come near you.
You say no less than what
you see, and nothing but
your eyes can hear you.

If "life's a dream with doubts
about itself," the dreaming
never stops.
                    Regretting
what you did or did not do
or always wished to do adds up
to who you are . . .
                        Piaf pretended
she regretted nothing.
                        One
genius in his epitaph regretted
only he was not "the man
in whose embrace Mathilde Urbach
swooned."
                    An emperor with no
regrets in middle age
regretted having no regrets.
Translated, these examples say
no life is long enough
nor cosmopolitan enough nor anything
enough.
                If you desire to see
your son's daughter's son's
daughter, you want no less
than anybody wants.
                        Or if you thirst
to visit everywhere in every
hemisphere, you mimic old Batuta's
passion for the next horizon.
Or if you hunger for the maximum,
you're Faust with all of Faust's
excesses to remember . . .
                            So much
for dreams.
                If you want something
to regret, why not regret you never
once opposed some fluent undermen   149

we manage to elect—the ideology
or sociology or therapy that people
eat as poetry—the arguments
about theology whose final argument
is *who's the boss*—the righteous
tribes for whom the Renaissance might
just as well have never happened.
Why did you never say that one
good student's worth a thousand
senators?
                    Or that one carpenter
outskills the slitherings of advertisers,
diplomats, and other oilers of the word?
Between what you remember
or presume, you're in translation
by whatever keeps translating April
into May, decisions into consequences,
fathers into sons, and you
into whatever.
                    I know
the circumstance.
                    I'm you,
and both of us keep planning
for tomorrow while we're turning
into yesterday.
                    What else
can we conclude except we grow
and die in place despite
our dreams?
                    What is our bounty
but the permanent impermanence
of breath, a shared invisibility,
a gift?
                    What is our peace
but stopping as we go and talking
for a while of that, just
that, translation to translation?

UNDERSTUDY

In a world of shadows, you're
    a shadow.
           Each shadow has
a name, and who it's called
is what it does: mechanic,
postman, dentist, President
of these United States, attorney,
acrobat.
           Some mornings
you become your shadow and forget
the self you are.
           Shadowing
shadows or by shadows shadowed,
you pretend all shadows mean
no more than what they mean
to you.
           What's hidden is the animal
within that laughs and bleeds,
luxuriates in kisses, mistakes
what satisfies for what completes,
and wonders how its death
will come and where and when.
You've played at shadows long enough
to know a man can die
of order.
           Under every uniforming
face, the life that Aristotle
understood and Shakespeare dramatized
and everybody dies of when it's time
just waits and waits to happen
as it must.
           The fate of islanders
occurs to you.
           For years their seas
seem sisterly.

It takes one hurricane
alone to make them ask
which sea is real—the smooth
Sargasso or the waves of nightmare.
The same for Texans.
                    After one
tornado they believe they live
thereafter by the grace of chance
or some indulgence of the wind.
But why go on?
                    Shadow
inside of shadow, the world's
a Chinese box you're always
opening and opening.
                    It proves
the poem of your life will happen
like a poem on a page.
                    It starts
when something else takes over.
Suddenly you're stopped.
                    It's noon,
and not a shadow inks the earth.
You come alive to everything:
    the way your fingers shake
    a hammer handle like a hand,
    the lure of her both breasts
    uplifted underwater, children
    singing in Spanish, the fluent
    silence of the mute.
                    You're both
within and yet above yourself,
and even so the time being
is turning into shadow.
                    Always
Utopian, you keep expecting

more and finding less.
                              You crave
    the last impossibilities that lovers
    crave—a world devoid
    of anything o'clock, freshness
    in perpetuity, a holiday from history.
Your shadow waits for you
    regardless.
                        It's like a suit
    you can't outwear and never
    will discard.
                        It wants
    to wear you now and afterward
    and in your grave.
                              You let it wait.

MEDITERRANEANS

Instead of lotus, you can eat
   croissants, brioche, baguettes,
   and all the pastries of the sun.
The beach is breasts.
                      Pharmacies
   sell nipplecream in toothpaste
   tubes.
          Beyond Tahiti Beach
   and Pampalone what's visible
   below the navel and above declares
   the final nudities are metaphysical,
   not physical.
                  "Voulez-vous un parasol?"
A palace named for Alexandra
   blocks the view Picasso
   savored of the sea in Cannes.
Lebanese outnumber Saudis
   ten to one, and Arabic's
   the second language on the Rue
   d'Antibes.
           "Unna min Djoun.
Killna hown min Djoun.
                 Lady
   Stanhope lived in Djoun."
A Greek chorus of parked
   yachts is rung with wakes
   from skimmers, cleavers, surfers.
Shucking their tanning mats,
   the swimmers wade, kick,
   crawl, propel themselves
   like frogs, or float log-flat
   in tandem.
              The sun paints
   everyone a tawny copper.
"Marvin and me are doing

Rome tomorrow.
                    One day
    for Rome, then half a day
    for Florence—that's enough."
The nudes that Gauguin painted
    in the real Tahiti made him wonder:
    "Where do we come from, what
    are we, where are we going?"
Here the tourists' answer is,
    "We come from where we come from,
    we're who our passports say
    we are, we're going home."
Under the stars the mistral scatters
    cellophane and kleenex on the sand.
The always-virgin waves seem strewn
    with coins or snow from the moon.
The sea is no one's country.

WHO PROMISED YOU TOMORROW?

It's time you paganized yourself
   and left all sublimations
   to the dry of soul.
                              It's time
   you learned that ears can taste,
   and eyes remember, and the tongue
   and nostrils see like fingertips
   in any dark.
                           Think back
   or look around, and all you know
   is what your body taught you:
   lake smoke in the Adirondacks,
   the razor's flame across
   your lathered cheek, language
   that changed to silence or to tears
   when there was nothing more
   to say . . .
                         Right here in Cannes
   on the Fourth of July, you watch
   a cornucopia a-swelter in the sun.
A Saudi wife, enrobed
   and cowled like a nun, passes
   a Cannaise in her isosceles
   and thong.
                      They stand there
   like opposed philosophies of women,
   history, desire, God,
   and everything you think about
   too much . . .
                       The stationed candles
   on the altar of Notre Dame
   de Bon Voyage diminish
   like your future.
                          Anchored
   in the bay, the *S.S. Ticonderoga*

claims the future's now.
Housing a zillion dollars'
   worth of software in her hull,
   she's programmed for the war
   that no one wants.
               She bristles
   like a plowshare honed into a sword—
   the ultra-weapon from the ultra-tool.
Basking in the hull of your skin
   that shields the software of yourself
   against the worst, you contemplate
   the carefully united states
   you call your body.
               Concealed
   or bared, it houses who you are,
   and who you are is why you live,
   and why you live is worth
   the life it takes to wonder how.
Your body's not concerned.
                It answers
   what it needs with breath, sleep,
   love, sweat, roses,
   children, and a minimum of thought.
It says all wars are waged
   by puritans, and that the war
   nobody wants is history's excuse
   for every war that ever happened . . .
The gray *Ticonderoga* fires
   a salute of twenty guns
   plus one for independence
   and the men who died to earn it.
Each shot reminds you of the killed
   Americans still left in France.
Before they left their bodies,
   did they think of war or what

their bodies loved and missed
the most: a swim at noon,
the night they kissed a woman
on her mouth, the dawns they waited
for the wind to rise like music,
or the simple freedom of a walk,
a waltz, a trip?
               Under
the sun of Cannes, you hum
your mind to sleep.
                   You tell
yourself that time is one
day long or one long day
with pauses for the moon and stars,
and that tomorrow's sun is yesterday's
today.
          Your body answers
that it knows, it's known
for years, it's always known.

FRENCH TIME

The French are like that . . .
—A REMARK EN PASSANT

Her equally tanned and equal
    breasts repeat the tawny russet
    of the tiles above her balcony.
Her white panties echo
    the whiteness of dreams.
                 No dream,
    she waters window-troughs
    of peonies, blow-dries her blonde
    hair, and never draws the blinds.
You're watching Wimbledon and her.
Wimbledon's losing.
           A Czech
    spartan and an unacclaimed Australian
    serve, volley, and slam
    for Lady Di and half the watching
    world.
       You watch *La Belle Evoque*
behind her peonies.
             She offers
what a woman's body offers:
curvatures, a special poise
in standing still, legs
like a dancer's, hair with its own
loose will, a shoulderblade
as rudimentary as a wing,
the inner secrecies.
          At Wimbledon,
Australia's rallying.
          When you
look back, *La Belle Evoque's*
abed.
      Beside her lies a man

with arms and shoulders of a stevedore.
A television signal flickers
   like a prairie fire across
   their touching tans.
                Australia's
   just a point away from triumph.
Suddenly in mid-lob the channel
   changes to commercials, news,
   and then John Wayne on horseback
   saying, *"Bonjour."*
             You focus
   on the prone-to-proneness game
   across the way.
             Starting at love,
   it's now advanced to deuce
   or, borrowing from French, *égalité.*
Out suddenly goes the prairie
   fire.
        Whatever's happening
   in darkness or on British grass
   dissolves behind the double fault
   of being unexplained and out
   of bounds.
           But this, you tell
   yourself, is France.
             No
   explanation is an explanation.
Point.
    Set.
       Match.

A MAN CAN THINK FOR JUST SO LONG BEFORE
THE BODY WANTS ITS SAY

It's not impressed with songs
    that won't stay past, with martyrs
    who will never die, with books
    forever speaking in the present
    tense.
           It lives on breezes
    that become its bones, on kisses
    that abandon it to slaveries
    that set it free, on water
    that reminds it of itself.
                            Give
    it a pear, and it's content.
Deliver it to roses, drumbeats,
    or the fresh truth of bread,
    and it will be your dog.
Why should it wait with you
    for what's to come or what's
    beyond or what's above
    if all its heavens are within?
It craves the immortalities of sense
    that keep a man undying
    while he lives.
                  Its every mouth
    speaks nothing but necessity.
Leave one unsatisfied, and it will
    peak in rages that can start
    a war, abolish populations
    in the name of need, defy
    impossibilities, and plunder hemispheres.
Yet always all it seeks is just
    the seesaw-peace of nature's algebra—
    the counterpoint between parfaits
    and pepper, itch and scratch,
    phantasmagoria and focus, babble

and song.
And what it feels
is yours to savor long before
the Platonist within you says
it's all unreal.
The problem is
it's not.
The signatures of pain
are legible as print.
And Maura's
eyes are unforgettable.
And loving
one who loves you back is more
electric than a trillion storms.
And healing, which you quietly
accept but can't explain,
is miracle enough to re-create
the universe . . .
Housed in your body's
universe, you make it
what it makes of you.
Pampered,
it softens.
Pressured, it toughens.
Summoned, it answers to a name
as long as answering is possible.
Sickened, it lingers to a close . . .
Its days are like a book
left open on a table in the wind.
The wind keeps reading all
its pages—faster, faster.

THE TIME IT TAKES TO SEE

This poem isn't working out.
I want to say that words
    and wonder stay at odds.
                    Feel
what you see when you see it,
and the sight's within you.
                       Speak,
and it's gone.
            Is it a mystery
to claim we aren't rehearsed
for mystery.
              When death or joy
or love surprises us, we end
by grieving, talking out of tune,
or looking idiotic.
               Years
afterward we find the words
for what we had no words for
then, which means the past
is simply what we make (re-make)
of it, which means we're always
in arrears.
             We sort our memories
like players who arrange the cards
they're dealt into a kind of order.
Failing even there, we say
that only artists save the minute
as it fades.
           Compared with all
the bronze perfections of Rodin,
we kiss like amateurs, have stances
that are less than statuesque,
and dance with all the dignity
of clowns.
           But why compare?

Rodin the sculptor knew
    the luxury of second sight
    and carved with all the flawlessness
    that retrospect allowed.
                    Rodin
    the man was like the rest of us,
    knowing the heart can never
    be prepared for what awaits it,
    knowing we do the best we can
    without the option of revision.
Is art mere taxidermy then,
    a way of re-inventing yesterday
    into the day we wanted it to be?
Or does the time of seeing
    happen when we revolutionize past
    wonder into something we can say?
One way or the other, seeing's
    not believing any more than
    listening means only hearing.
Somehow the time at hand
    must come again when we're
    composed enough to understand.
If what we've lost by then
    to living we've regained in gratitude,
    we've lost as ably as we can.

IN A TIME OF NO ANSWERS

If we're like rivers only love
    or suffering can stop for just
    so long, we deepen where we stop
    the longest.
                Afterward we're less
    self-consciously but more ourselves.
We consecrate our words.
                    We walk
    like acolytes.
              We see in all
    we see a prophecy of disappearance.
A nightgown flung like a spent
    lung across a bed sings mutely
    of absence.
              The slow dying
    of old snow remembers how
    we watched it burn from blizzards
    into thaw.
              Careers, distinctions,
    birthdays, and the rest dissolve
    like smoke-words scrawled
    by Piper Cubs across the sky.
Outwardly, we're what we were.
Because today's denial is tomorrow's
    truth, we still distrust all versions
    dubbed official.
              We see
    the owl of Minerva fly
    at dusk, which means philosophers
    philosophize when epochs end,
    not helpfully before.
              We watch
    as priests become the butlers of God
    while poets remain God's prodigal
    sons, forgivable at last

despite excesses in the name
of love.
                    Regardless, the world
of no retreat and no alternative
still stabs us with itself.
Each time we rise from loving,
    satisfied but never quite content,
    we feel the wound.
                            Speaking,
spoken to, or spoken of, we live
like actors at odd jobs
between plays.
                    We wonder if the jobs
or plays are real.
                    As actors we admit
    that skill is greater than strength,
    and art is greater than skill,
    and life is greater than art.
But after that we stop.
Even as the river in us
    tugs us on, we want
    to see the unforeseeable.
We search and search until
    we learn that living best
    means doing what we must with no
    foreknowledge of the outcome.
                                Where
    we are and whom we love
    and how we've come this far
    is all we know.
                    The time
    at hand is immortality enough.
It calls us like a road
    that leads to everything, and so
    we listen for directions, and we go.

AFTER MERCUTIO

Come we to this commemoration
   nude or garbed, we stay
   in most ways one.
                Midnight
enshrouds us, and the moon berobes us
   gray and silver to the galaxies.
Black lawns await the sun
   to paint them green again.
The sick are for a time sleep-spared
   the cruelty of roses.
                Swimming
a sweeter dark, a lover
   lets his fingertips be eyes
   until the lolling one he teases
   sheaths and thighs him to herself.
The kiss of bellies is their
   everything.
          Elsewhere in the easy
cladding of her skin, a showered
   wife looks west.
             Whatever
she's observing is composing her.
Cats are afoot.
         Their arch
   stares sparkle sapphire
   in the shadows.
           Listen.
             Volcanoes
   in the sea are spewing ash.
We overhear them as the deaf
   hear detonations with their eyes.
Chocked attics whisper
   to themselves like thieves in corridors.
Isled in the sunlight of the seafall
   moon, we beachcomb where we choose
   while everything around us
   turns into itself.

Because
a willow wavers, we believe
in wind, believe in stars
ensorcelled by the same wind,
believe ourselves believing.
We praise the perfect poem
of a hen's each egg.
                    Platters
of wet grapes in loose
erotic sprawls seem irresistible
as kisses.
              Rivers arouse
and reach within us oceans
far beyond our fathoming.
When we're made mad enough
by all this sorcery, we dance
fandangos on the shore before
we sleep.
              Or else we sing
the hymm that David sang to Saul
until the old king woke
and walked.
                  The world deserves
that little . . .
                  Nightwords
like these are not for those
who love the lies of triumph
that prevail as history.
                          They're
for the fools who pry from mystery
some memory of who we are
and why we're here.
                        They're for
the mildly bemused and wildly
free.
          For you.
For me.

TO ALL MY MARINERS IN ONE

Forget the many who talk
   much, say little, mean
   less and matter least.
                   Forget
we live in times when broadcasts
of Tchaikovsky's Fifth precede
announcements of the death
of tyrants.
              Forget that life
   for governments is priced
   war-cheap but kidnap-high.
Our seamanship is not with such.
From port to port we learn
   that "depths last longer
   than heights," that years are
   meant to disappear like wakes,
   that nothing but the sun stands
   still.
      We share the sweeter
   alphabets of laughter and the slower
   languages of pain.
                Common
   as coal, we find in one another's
   eyes the quiet diamonds
   that are worth the world.
                   Drawn
   by the song of our keel, who
   are we but horizons coming true?
Let others wear their memories
   like jewelry.
             We're of the few
   who work apart so well
   together when we must.
               We speak
   cathedrals when we speak

and trust no promise but
the pure supremacy of tears.
                            What
more can we expect?
                    The sea's
blue mischief may be waiting
for its time and place, but still
we have the stars to guide us.
We have the wind for company.
We have ourselves.
                    We have
a sailor's faith that says
not even dying can divide us.

ANOTHER WORD FOR TIME

We speak as people in motion
   speak, more sure of what's
   behind us than ahead,
   but going anyway.
                    Trying to see
beyond the world we see,
   we see that seeing's dangerous.
Our props collapse.
                Religion,
   custom, law, the dream
   called government . . .
                  Nothing
sustains us but our eyes and what
our eyes, by saying nothing,
say.
    No wonder Timmerman
could claim for all of us,
"I am at home in subjects
now, not countries."
                 Before
the real frontiers, our passports
are invalid.
              They tell us
how we're called but never
who we are, and who we are's
the mystery.
               The pilgrim in us
has no fixed address.
                 He roams.
He takes us with him when
   he goes.
             Encowled within
a fuselage, we speed toward
a short tomorrow in another
world.

We land, speak languages
we almost understand, and trust
in strangers as the best of friends,
and for a time they are.
                              Years
afterward we feel a bond
with them so indestructible
that we're amazed.
                              If they
should die, we'd grieve for them
like those old Cuban fishermen
who grieved for Hemingway because
he fished the gulf they fished
and called them friends.
                              With nothing
else to offer him, they gave
the bronze propellers of their
very boats for melting to create
his statue in the plaza of Cojimar . . .
For us the best memorials
are what we heard or read
en route.
                              "He's old, but still
in life."
                              "Nothing but heart
attack kill Christophine, but why
in the box she so swell up?"
"Cruelty's a mystery and a waste
of pain."
                              "I like a dog
that makes you think when you
look at him."
                              *"El Cordobés es
un hombre muy valiente."*
                              Each word's

a time.
                    Each time's a place.
Each place is where a time
    repeats itself because a word
    returns us there.
                        Crisscrossing
    through the universe the way
    that lightning diagrams the sky,
    we're all companions of the road
    at different altitudes.
                        Here
    in my speeding house below
    the speeding stars, I'm turning
    into language from a pen while you're
    confiding in some traveler you'll
    never see again.
                        The quiet
    bronze of words remembers us.
                            It says
    we were, we are, we will be.

THE REAL REASON FOR GOING IS NOT JUST TO GET THERE

For Anne Mullin Burnham

Killarney's maps are for the unredeemed.
The hidden land awaits the stumblers
    and the temporarily confused who find
    their destinations as they go.
In Dingle there's a history
    bone-final as the faith
    that founded Gallarus.
                     All
    that survives is what was there
    when Gallarus began: God,
    man, sheep, and stone
    and stone and stone.
                 Dingles
    ago, the starvers saw their lips
    turn green from chewing grass
    before they famished in their beds.
Their hovels bleach like tombs
    unroofed and riven by the sea.
If only all the stones were beige
    or marble-white . . .
                 The fading
    grays seem unforgiving as a fate
    that only wit or tears
    or emigration can defeat.
Sheep graze over graves.
Loud gulls convene on garbage
    dumps.
          In Galway, Cashel,
    and Tralee, I fish the air
    for what it is that makes
    the Irish Irish.
               Is it Seamus

speaking Sweeney's prayer
in Howth and telling me of Hopkins,
"the convert," buried in Glasnevin?
Is it how it sounds to sing
the music in a name: Skibbereen,
Balbriggan, Kilbeggan, Bunratty,
Listowel, Duncannon, Fermanagh,
and Ballyconneely?
                              Is it Joyce's
map of metaphors that makes
all Dublin mythical as Greece?
Is it cairns of uniambic and unrhyming
rocks transformed by hand
into the perfect poem of a wall?
Is it the priest near death
who whispered, "Give my love
to Roscommon, and the horses
of Roscommon"?
                              Is it because
the Irish pray alike for "Pope
John Paul, our bishop Eamon, and
Ned O'Toole, late of Moycullen"?
Inside God's house or out
their sadder smiles say the world,
if given time, will break your heart.
With such a creed they should
believe in nothing but the wisdom
of suspicion.
                              Instead they say,
"Please God," and fare ahead
regardless of the odds to show
that life and God deserve at least
some trust, some fearlessness, some courtesy.

WHATEVER HAPPENED TO DEFIANCE?

People you will never want to know
  are telling you to vote, enlist,
  invest, travel to Acapulco,
  buy now and pay later, smoke,
  stop smoking, curb your dog,
  remember the whale, and praise
  the Lord.
            Like windshield wipers
  they repeat themselves.
                        Because
  they tell but never ask, you learn
  to live around them just to live.
You understand why Paul Gauguin
  preferred Tahiti to the bourgeoisie
  of France.
            But then Tahiti's
  not the answer anymore,
  and frankly never was.
                    This leaves
  you weighing Schulberg's waterfront
  philosophy: "You do it to him
  before he does it to you."
Reactionary, you admit, but nature's
  way, the way of this world
  where he who wins is always
  he who loses least and last . . .
But if you're bored by triumph
  through attrition, imitate you may
  the strategy of Puck.
                    Listen
  carefully to all solicitations, smile,
  and respond in classical Greek.
It's devious, but then it gives
  you time to smell the always
  breathing flowers.

          Or to watch
dissolve into the mystery of coffee
the faceless dice of sugar
cubes.
          Or to say how damn
remarkable it is that every
evening somewhere in this world
a play of Shakespeare's being staged
with nothing to be won but excellence.

ON THE EVE OF THE FIRST SHOT

I've never seen so many generals,
    and none in uniform.
                    This general
    talks nuclear.
                    This general predicts.
This general's for royalty and oil-ty.
This general's too fat.
                    He breathes
    like something leaking air.
This general says do it now
    or do it later, but, for God's
    sake, do it . . .
                    Mothers are silent.
Fathers are silent.
                    Young
    wives who kiss their husbands
    on the docks are silent.
                    Elsewhere
    in studios, on radio, in stereo,
    the generals are noisy with solutions.
No one can silence them.
After the war, they'll
    tell us all the same
    predictions in reverse, proving
    the war developed as they said,
    with due allowance for the deals,
    the drudgery, the dollars, and the dead.

WAR NEWS VIEWED IN THE TROPICS

It seems like melodrama beamed
    from Mars: two Presidents like goats
    about to butt, marines in bunkers
    reading every letter's every word,
    tank captains squinting
    from their turrets "somewhere in Arabia."
Among mimosa, bougainvillea,
    and coconuts, what sucks me back
    into this nausea for news?
                         Remembering
    Seferis, I can say my country
    wounds me anywhere I go.
What's happening to us?
Is this how America's century
    ends?
           Why are we now
    so quick to kill however slowly
    and so slowly quick to sweat
    for peace?
               For months we've acted
    like the new crusaders, righteous
    as Barbarossa and the British kings.
The true cross of our cause
    is true for everyone
    because we say it is.
Not that we're trapped between
    a tyrant and a sheik with eighty
    sons.
          Not that we've bought
    accomplices we call allies.
                    Not that
    the sand will claim our camps
    as surely as the years made wrecks
    of Richard's castles near the coast.
Not that we've made a hoax

of history . . .

Meanwhile, old Moscow's
come apart like Rome, Constantinople,
and Madrid.

Eleven-time-zones
wide, all Russia begs
like Ethiopia for bread.

The second
world's careening into bits.
Here in the third, the islanders
respond to our new order
with their own.

They've started
hoarding kerosene.

They pray
unhopefully for peace.

They say
the worst is always unforeseen.

THE VOW WE BREATHE

It's not the years.
                    What
are they but a way (and not
the best) to count the past?
And what's the past but who
    we've grown to be right now?
And how can that make life
    more sacred or an inch
    less dangerous?
                    Our rooms
gaze out on flowers that proclaim
like flags we're here to be
each other's counterpart, and that's
enough.
                    And yet to live
together but to die alone
seems so unjust of God
the merciful.
                    The mate who's left
goes on but partially, unable
or unwilling to disguise the naked
limp of being incomplete.
The Greeks were wrong.
                    Those
whom the gods would destroy
they make at first not mad,
but happy.
                    What else
is tragedy, is life?
                    If I
could make a toast, I'd say
each breath and not each year's
an anniversary.
                    Your rhododendrons
say that every time they bloom.

And so do all your hyacinths,
   azaleas, tulips, dogwoods,
   lilacs, and wisterias.
                     Because
of you I bless these blossoms
by their names.
              I bless this true
and holy earth that undergirds
us while we live and hides
us when we die.
             I bless
all love that baffles understanding,
human or divine.
            What else
explains how every mate's
a lock one key alone
can open?
         I'm yours.
             You're mine.

LOVEMAKERS

Loves mysteries in soules do grow,
but yet the body is his booke.
                                        —JOHN DONNE

It's what you feel when you
        become a poem, and you reach
        to sing yourself to her
        whose presence has created you.
Your very lips are words.
                                Your hands
        speak sentences.
                                Your body
        learns a language it is just
        inventing, touch by touch . . .
She turns from being merely
        naked to the Modigliani nude
        that every woman changes to,
        aroused.
                        Her breasts forget
        their future.
                                She thinks so
        softly with her thighs that not
        a ripple stirs the surfaces
        she swims . . .
                                Like figure-skating
        or the last duet from *La Boheme*
        or two in tandem on a bike,
        this double solo will decline
        from ecstasy to prose with one
        mistake.
                        Its moments match
        the slow infinity of clouds.
It shows how one plus one
        make one in the first,
        the best, the ultimate of dances.

Later—but much too soon—when
   bodies slacken back to fact,
   the sea becomes its sheeted
   self again, and all the unrepentant
   and abolished clocks reclaim
   a time that for a moment scorned them.

ONE FLESH

All those who wrote of loving,
    even Shakespeare, missed the point.
Describing lips, hair, eyebrows,
    breasts, and thighs is not
    enough.
            All this is merely
    what's observable, and love
    outraces the observable as sight
    outraces sound across the universe.
When observation stops and lovers
    act, they are what words
    attempt to say and, saying,
    fail to say.
            The alphabet
    of lovers speaks in pauses,
    touches, cries, and tears
    involuntary as a blink and just
    as uncontrollable.
                        It sails
    them through the night
    as dreams might sail them
    through wing-feather sleep.
It's more than being free
    of underwear and watches, more
    than the stiffening and sheathing
    flesh that lets them bind and bond
    and be what Plato claimed we were
    in the beginning, more even than
    the ecstasies of luck or God
    or ecstasy itself.
                It leaves them
    animal enough just long
    enough to learn the language
    of the tiger and the lamb.
                        But while

they're one another, they become
a land that no one's mapped
though most have tried—a song
that must be sung to be
the song it is—a time
so free of time that nothing
matters but donating to each other
everything they are . . .

                      Spent,
they disengage and lie together
in the loll of after-love
and listen.

            The walls, the air,
the bed become so quietly
important.

            White curtains
ripple like the hushed flags
of peace.

         An over-flying jet
pursues its decrescendo over lights
and silences as reassuring as the stars.

HOW MARRIED PEOPLE ARGUE

Because they disagreed on nuclear
    disarmament, because he'd left
    the grass uncut, because she'd spilled
    a milkshake on his golfbag,
    he raced ten miles faster
    than the limit.
                    Stiffening,
    she scowled for him to stop it.
His answer was to rev it up
    to twenty.
                    She asked him why
    a man of his intelligence would
    take out his ill-temper on a car?
He shouted in the name of Jesus
    that he never ever lost
    his damn temper.
                    She told him
    he was shouting—not to shout—
    that shouting was a sign of no
    intelligence.
                    He asked a backseat
    witness totally invisible
    to anyone but him why women
    had to act like this.
                    She muttered
    "Men," as if the word were mouthwash
    she was spitting in a sink.
                    Arriving
    at the party, they postponed the lethal
    language they were saving for the kill
    and played "Happily married."
Since all the guests were gorging
    on chilled shrimp, the fake went
    unobserved.
                    She found a stranger's

jokes so humorous she almost
choked on her martini.
                      He demonstrated
for the hostess how she could
improve her backswing.
                      All the way
home they played "Married
and so what."
                      She frowned as if
the car had a disease.
                      He steered
like a trainee, heeding all
speed limits to the letter,
whistling, "Some Enchanted Evening"
in the wrong key, and laughing
in a language only he could
understand.
                      At midnight, back
to back in bed, he touched
the tightness of her thigh.
                      She muttered,
"I'm asleep," as if her permanent address
were sleep.
                      He rose and roamed
the darkened house, slammed
every door he passed, and watched
a prison film with George Raft.
Abed at dawn, he heard
the tears she meant for him
to hear.
                      He listened and lay still.
Because they both had round-trip
tickets to the past but only
one-way tickets to the future,
he apologized for both of them.

They waited for their lives to happen.
He said the hostess's perfume
   was Eau de Turpentine.
                     She said
   the party was a drag—no humor.
Word by word, they wove themselves
   in touch again.
              Then silence
   drew them close as a conspiracy
   until whatever never was
   the issue turned into the nude
   duet that settled everything
   until the next time.

TWO AGAINST THE MOUNTAIN

Surely you have seen us
    spidering our way from piton
    to piton up sheer rock,
    trusting only in our feet
    and fingers and the rope of life
    between us.
                We're certain
    of our goal but not the route.
That's something we discover
    inch by inch by listening
    to what the mountain knows.
With both our lives at stake,
    we make a wedding out of work.
Now and again—a word . . .
Otherwise . . . the slow strain
    of reaching sideward to be sure
    before we step but still unsure
    until the step is taken.
Those moments when the outcome
    is in doubt is why we climb.
Connected, we become what
    those who keep each other's
    life in trust become.
                Who knows
    the word for this?
                It's waging
    both our lives on faith
    by pitting all we are against
    what cannot be foretold.
It's falling when we fail
    but knowing that whatever held
    or holds the two of us together
    like a vow will hold, will hold.

THE YEAR OF THE HORSE

My father said, "All horses
    when they run are beautiful."
I think of that each time
    I watch Arabians in silhouette,
    the clobbering drays, the jet
    stallions that policemen rein,
    the stilting foals and colts, the sometimes
    bumping always pumping rumps
    of geldings harnessed to a rig.
They prance through war and history:
    "Without the horse the Mongols
    never could have conquered Europe."
And tragedy: "A horse, a horse,
    my kingdom for a horse!"
And sport: "Five minutes
    of hard polo will exhaust
    the strongest horse on earth."
Unsaddled and afoot, how far
    could Cossack, cowboy, Indian,
    and cavalier have gone?
                    What made
    so many generals and emperors
    prefer their portraiture on horseback?
What simulacrum but a horse
    succeeded where Achilles failed?
And where did John put hatred,
    famine, pestilence, and war
    but on the backs of horses?
                    And that's
    not all.
          Pegasus still says
to gravity that poetry's none
other than a horse with wings.
It's not a question of intelligence.
Horses, like poetry, are not

intelligent—just perfect
in a way that baffles conquest,
drama, polo, plow,
and shoe.
    So poem-perfect
that a single fracture means
a long, slow dying in the hills
or, if man's around, the merciful
aim an inch below the ear.
But when they run, they make
    the charge of any boar at bay,
    the prowl of all the jungle
    cats, the tracking beagle,
    or the antelope in panic seem
    ignoble.
        Just for the sake
of the running, the running, the running
they run . . .
            And not another
animal on two or four
or forty legs can match
that quivering of cords beneath
their pelts, the fury in their manes,
the hooves that thump like rapid
mallets on the earth's mute drum,
the exultation of the canter and the gallop
and the rollick and the frolic and the jump.

Whatever you can buy's not valuable
    enough, regardless of the cost.
What can't be bought's invaluable.
Not just the white freedom
    of a rose, sparrows in their soaring
    circuses, that girl from Amsterdam
    so tanly tall in Montfleury,
    harbors at noon with clouds
    above them pillowing like snow
    and absolutely still.
                      I'm talking
love.
      I'm talking love
and poetry and everything that's true
of each and interchangeably of both.
Randomly free, they leave
    us grateful to no giver
    we can name.
                They prove what cannot
    last can last forever even
    when we say it's lost . . .
Some losers ache like Aengus
    or like Leila's madman, pining
    for a time so briefly given
    and so quickly gone.
                Bereft,
    they raise their anguish into songs
    that give a tongue to wounds
    that never heal.
             In every song
    they imitate those troubadours
    whose poems have outlived
    their lives.
          Forget how far
    they went in school, their ages,

or their kin.
                    Whatever wanted
to be said and wanted only them
to say it made them what
they are.
                    It turned them
into words that we can share
like bread and turn into ourselves.
They asked, as I am asking now,
    for some less unforgiving way
    to say it, and there isn't.
Or if what happened once
    might be repeated, and it can't.
Or if another poet's words
    would say it better, and they don't.
Or if this cup could pass
    and spare them poetry and all
    its contradictions, and it won't.

STINGERS

Sluggish and tame, October's
   bees inspect the space
   between my elbow and my pipe.
I welcome the distraction . . .
                      So much
   around me's changed.
                My first
   time here the Tigers won
   the flag and spared Detroit
   from being torched a second
   time.
       Today the city's
   down a million, sliding
   westward, and the skyline
   flattens into crabgrass-lots
   that once were neighborhoods.
When anyone suggests Detroit
   is prototypical, the mayor
   swears on television . . .
                  Still
   they count the yearly murders
   here the way the Goodyear
   meter totals day by day
   an endless birth of tires.
Earlier I asked a friend,
   "What's your response to urban
   violence?"
             "I keep my pistol
 loaded."
        This from a doctor
   of status, taste, and means
   but with a mind too fortified
   to think.
        Why didn't I say
   that weapons are the spawn of fear,

that fortress-minds—like all
the forts in history—are destined
for defeat, that waiting for the worst
allows the worst to happen?
My questions circle me like bees
that may at any moment strike.
The real bees dip and dawdle
in the sun.
                    They seem bemused.
They let me live in their environment,
not mine.
                    In time they'll do
what bees must do and sting.
The poison's there and waiting.

PUTTING AWAY THE LOST SUMMER

The swing's unslung and winter-waxed,
    the mint leaves waiting to be sieved
    to salt, the hose unscrewed
    and coiled like a rattler in the shed.
As usual the ripening figs
    will blacken at first frost
    exactly as they did last year
    when all the talk was war.
This year the human harvest
    makes the war seem dim:
    one suicide, three deaths, one
    shock, one disappointment, and a swindle.
Each one bequeathed its epitaph:
    "Your letter was a narrow bridge
    to the rest of my life."
                        "He didn't
    recognize me, Sam—his own
    sister."
            "I'll stay until he's well
    or else not here anymore."
Remembering, I see how much
    can never be the way it was,
    despite appearances.
                        Philosophy's
    no help.
            Religion's even less.
And poetry does nothing but re-live
    what's lost without redeeming it
    like life's exact revenge
    upon itself.
                What's left
    but learning to survive with wounds?
Or studying the fate of figs
    before the unexpected chill,
    not knowing in advance how many

or how few will be destroyed
or toughened when it comes . . .
Playing for time, I occupy
myself with chores and tools,
uncertain if the lot I've chosen
is a gambler's or a coward's or a fool's.

You think of photographic paper
   drowning in developer.
              Slowly
   the whiteness darkens into forms.
Shadows become a face;
   the face, a memory; the memory,
   a name.
         The final clarity
   evolves without a rush
   until it's there.
          It's like
   your struggle to remember
   what you know you know
   but just can't quite recall.
No matter how you frown,
   the secret stays beyond you.
You reach.
       It moves.
            You reach
  again.
       Again it moves.
It's disobedience itself, but still
   it wants so much to be regained
   by you, only by you.
            Later,
   when it lets itself be known,
   you wonder how you ever could
   have lost so obvious a thing.
And yet you take no credit
   for retrieving it.
           It came to you
  on its own terms, at its
  own time.
       You woke, and it
  was there like love or luck

or life itself and asked
no more of you than knowing
it by name.
                    The name is yours
to keep.
          You burn to share
this sudden and surprising gold
with everyone.
                    You feel the glee
of being unexpectedly complete
and sure and satisfied and chosen.

AT MIDNIGHT THERE ARE NO HORIZONS

I

The suckle-skin that slakes
   the smallest thirst is fed
   by what is sucking it.
                  Tightly
   bonded at the loins, all lovers
   flex and thrust in ditto
   ravenings they rouse
   and satisfy and, satisfying, rouse
again.
        Pre-skeletal, we're
   at the mercy of our mouths.
Or are we merely one
   another's food as God is ours?
Beneath the world of the polite,
   the meekly conscientious or the quietly
   predictable, we vie with deeper
   hungers.
            Hungering, we're like a bride
   who shucks her slip and under-
   silks and lets herself be loved
   into a new geography.
                Her final
   whimpers wake her like a field
   that lightning suddenly ignites
   into the height and depth and breadth
   of what it means to *be*.
            Or
   we can rise like Cain and kill
   a brother who will be no less
   a brother in his grave.
             What good's
   philosophy if what we are
   is what we are?

How holy
are religions if we've killed for God
as readily as for revenge
or jealousy or just the hell of it?
On days as brief as pleasure
or as long as sorrow, we concede
as feeder or as food that all civility's
a lie, and everything from love
to murder is a twitch of appetite.

2

Death hides in every clock,
and so we damn them all.
They keep reverting us to bone
or else to relics that re-live us . . .
Dour drunk deadman's gone
to the angels.
Gone too
the southern cavalier who sang
of war and bats and what
it meant to wither.
Gone
last the lanky king
who lorded wide his royalty
by cunning, craft, and kin
until he paced the stage alone.
What are they now but pages
on a small, tight shelf of books?
Each one keeps to his inches.

3

Clockmakers from Ticino say
    that every minute wounds us,
    and the last one kills.
                        Wounded
    every day but still undead,
    we breathe behind last words—
    "All else being equal . . ." or "Nine
    chances out of ten . . ." or "Barring
    the unforeseeable."
                        We learn
    too late that nothing's equal
    here, that single chances are the most
    we get, that everything is unforeseeable.
The poem of our lives proclaims
    there's something still ahead
    to be discovered if we just have time.
Rush, and we miss it.
                        Wait,
    and it finds us.
                        Even
    while we notch initials in a birch,
    have schools or sons or streets
    named after us, endow cathedrals
    to remember us in bronze, the poem
    of our lives is always being
    born.
                    We are the picture
    it's creating, breath by breath.
What's taking shape is never
    what we planned and not what we expect.
We call it life because we must.
We have it just where it wants us.

SOLDIERS DESPITE OURSELVES

Downstairs a trumpeter is playing
   Gershwin badly but somehow
   truer that way.
                The squat
   chimney of my pipe keeps offering
   smoke-signals to the moon.
The sea-waves glitter like a zillion
   nickels . . .
             Two wars ago
   the battle of the Riviera happened
   here.
        Two wars ago
   the author of *The Little Prince*
   flew southward from this coast
   and crashed at sea without a trace.
That's how I tell the time
   these days—by wars, the madness
   of wars.
           I think of Mussolini,
   who believed each generation
   needed war to purify its blood.
He leaned on history to show
   that life's unlivable except
   through death.
             I palm the ashes
   from my pipe.
          To hell
   with Mussolini.
            I'll take
   bad Gershwin to a bullet
   any time.
          To hell with history.
The moon's manna on the sea
   outshines the glory that was Greece.
To hell with those who say

the earth's a battleground we're doomed
to govern with a gun.
                              Because
of them we have to fight to live.
But win or lose, they've won
     since fighting proves they're right.
Why ask if they outnumber us
     or not?
               It just takes one.

MATADOR

He killed dying, and he died killing.
—TRANSLATION OF THE HEADLINE
ANNOUNCING THE DEATH OF MANOLETE,
AUGUST 28, 1948

Are my eyes open, Doctor? I can't see.
—LAST WORDS OF MANOLETE

The photographs survive.
                              He stood
    at sentinel's attention in his suit
    of lights.
                    His cape encowled him
    like a crimson wing.
                              Kneeling
    before the snout or kissing
    the horn of a bled and broken
    bull he thought undignified.
                                        Instead
    he faced the black fury
    of the beast at full strength,
    steering him from miss to miss
    until the sacrifice.
                              His art
    was not to fight but to conduct
    the bull the way a maestro
    might conduct an orchestra.
                                        With death
    as close as God or love,
    he worked his cape like a baton
    and never moved his feet . . .
He never moved his feet.
No wonder they revere his melancholy
    courage to this very day
    in Córdoba, Madrid, and Mexico.
And they have reason.

Even
the ones who hate the spectacle
respect the man who braved so
much without a backward step.
Forget the fame, the mistress,
and the fortune in pesos.
                              Can these
explain why someone heeds
a calling that allows as many
victories as possible but only
one defeat?
                    What each of us
evades until the end, he faced
six hundred times alone
by choice.
                    Six hundred times . . .
His final bull surprised him
even as he stabbed and left him
crumpled, gored, and bleeding
on the sand.
                    That memory
is ours to swallow like the bread
of sorrow and the wine of contradiction.
It shows that valor's a delaying
action after all.
                    If done
with grace, we praise the artistry
and skill.
                    If not, we say
the unexpected is the way
life always overrules us
in the name of life.
                    And life
can spare.
                    And life can kill.

ONCE AGAINST A TIME

1

Who said that life and being busy
        are the same?
                        Action for the Greeks
        meant thinking through and for
        the body.
                        What counted was the thought.
The act resulted like a good
        lieutenant following an order . . .
For those who need assignments
        or a cause to live, who dedicate
        themselves to institutions,
        or who network out their days,
        this makes no sense.
                        They think
        that life is what they don't
        yet have.
                        It's there, out there . . .
Contacts will make it possible,
        and so they burn their years
        connecting, re-connecting, unconnecting.
Where does it end?
                        And what's
        at stake?
                        And where's the competition?

2

If life's a heaven that's
        within us, what's the rush
        to seek it anywhere but there?
Why act as if we're not original
        and irreplaceable?

Each time
I watch old films of Wilma
Rudolph in a race, I have
to swallow tears.
                    Not that
she ran and won, but that
her strides were perfect, sure,
and absolutely hers.
                    Like Hemingway's
best prose for Hemingway.
Like Giacometti's naked pilgrims
marching straight to God.
                         It's not
sheer excellence that matters
here.
        It's how that excellence
returns us to a world
we've overlooked . . .
                    The reassuring
flatness of a floor.
                    The steady
sadness in a dog's small face.
The profile of a woman weeping
in the rain.
            Whether the water
on her cheeks is from her eyes
or from the clouds is not important.
What counts is what is there just once
before it vanishes.
                    If that's
forgettable, we're all forgettable.

FOR BILL

No one but you could write,
    "Our Father Who art in Heaven
    can lick their Father Who art
    in Heaven."
              After we laughed,
we saw all wars from Troy
    to Vietnam in those two lines.
You had that gift of turning
    smiles into thoughts in such
    a quiet, Quaker way.
              And yet
the saying stayed so casual
and conversational and untranslatably
Bill Stafford.
              I still remember
when we read in Michigan
together—you from a spiral
notebook crammed with short
poems in longhand.
              Listening,
I strove to spot where the poems
stopped, and the prose began.
I never found the seam . . .
When you wrote *Someday, Maybe,*
    what was it you were telling us?
If it was loss, that day
    was yesterday.
              You finished polishing
a poem that would be your last,
stood up to help your wife,
and fell like a soldier.
              As endings
go, that seems regrettably
acceptable.
              But why does it

remind me of the silence following
a poem's final line?
I want the poem to go on
    forever, but it doesn't.

                        And it does.

FOR TOMAS, WHO SURVIVED THE AXE BLOW FROM WITHIN

The darkening space in my projectile
    lightens with the voice of a great
    poet speaking his Swedish
    poems in English.
                In fact
    he's speechless, strangled by a stroke
    so that the only voice
    that's his is this one on a tape . . .
I see him blanketed near Stockholm,
    waiting for Monica, thinking
    of midsummer in the archipelago.
If dreams were words, I'd tell
    this man how much I need
    his poems and how true they are.
They heal like sacraments.
                Instead,
    I watch the road before me
    change into the road behind me
    like a threat faced once and then
    forgotten.
            The poems fill
    the car like Schubert at his best.
They guide me like a compass
    to a home far truer
    than the one I'm heading for.
Which takes more bravery—to live
    with words that never can be said
    or steer through Pennsylvania
    darkness in the rain?
                "His humor
    is wonderful, so we are more close
    than ever."
             These words were Monica's
    last year, and I repeat them

to the darkness, word by word.
Meanwhile, the tape reverses,
   and I let it play.
             The compass
steadies to a truer north
than north.
           It says that "patience
is love at rest," and love
means everything.
             Beside such certitude
I seem a man without virtue.

My father said, "Your work
    is never over—always
    one more page."
               This
from a traveling man whose life
was always one more mile . . .
I told him that.
             "Sometimes
I hate the road," he said,
"it's made me so I'm never
happy in one place.
          Don't
you get started."
            I never did,
spending my days in universities,
my nights at home.
          Not
typically the academic, not
totally at home at home,
I think of how I could have lived
and come up blank.
          What's
better than sharing all you know
and all you don't with students
who do just the same?
          Even
on the worst of days it justifies
the time.
          Or inking out
your real future on white
paper with a fountain pen
and listening to what the writing
teaches you?
          Compared to walking
on the moon or curing polio,

it seems so ordinary.
                    And it is.
But isn't living ordinary?
For two and fifty summers
    Shakespeare lived a life
    so ordinary that few scholars
    deal with it.
                And what of Faulkner
    down in ordinary Oxford, Mississippi?
Or Dickinson, the great recluse?
Or E. B. White, the writer's
    writer?
            Nothing extraordinary
    there, but, God! what wouldn't
    we give for one more page?

TO WATCH WITH LOVE'S EYES

Seeing begins when something
   looked at looks looked at.
It's not the same as recognition.
Show me a photo long enough,
   and it will memorize itself
   like a phone number dialed
   to the point of reflex.
               But seeing
   those you love asleep
   is seeing them dead or all
   at once more totally alive
   than you can bear.
            They seem
   without defenses—sinless—afloat.
Their breathing makes you think
   of breath as more than air—
   mere air.
          Who cares if nature
   seethes with unmalicious violence?
Or if all good and evil
   starts and ends with us,
   just us?
         Compared to breath,
   such questions seem so trivial.
And like them, all philosophy.
You want to damn to hell
   whatever says that life's
   a transmigration or a pointless fight
   where everybody loses in the end.
Even if it's true, so what?
There still are moments
   when the blessing of attention
   sanctifies a face as unrepeatable
   as breath itself.
           Where else

does love become a rose
that's not at odds with any
other rose in sight or out of sight?
We're moved to give, appreciate,
   forgive.
           And we're revived
   beyond our understanding or capacity
   like plants that must be drowned to live.

WHAT WAITS FOR US?

Take history.
             What is it
but a way we try but fail
to understand what's past?
It says what we consider vague
is definite because "it hasn't
finished happening yet."
As for the present, it deceives
us like a dream where all
our hungers speak.
                      Right now
we breathe.
                      Right now we chew.
Right now we mate.
                      Right now
we drink . . .
                      But that true fake
we call the future keeps seducing
us with promises.
                      We're driven
to expect, expect, expect.
And every expectation tells us
only what we choose to know.
But let's be frank.
                      The future's
never one more year to live
but one less year of what
remains.
             It lies.
                      It contradicts.
Consider Tomas mute and lame
in Scandinavia.
                      Two years ago
he was complete.
                      Or Andy, who collapsed

while dancing with his wife.
                              Or Joan,
who woke to find her house blazing.
Who knows when he awakes if he
    will sleep a murderer, a lover,
    or a fool?
              Regardless, we grope on,
    remembering the world ahead
    as if it were the world behind.
We struggle to regain what children
    do without a thought.
                              They live,
just live.
              It changes nothing.
Still, what matters more while we
    live yesterday today
    and face tomorrow's verdicts blind?

THE FUTURE IS THE PAST, READ BACKWARD

There is one question only. Will we live
forever or not?   —MIGUEL DE UNAMUNO

All those who made you possible
    two centuries ago have blurred.
Go back another thousand
    years, and everything's a guess.
But here you stand in the present
    tense—alert and shamelessly
    the center of a world named you . . .
Imagine now you're in the next
    millennium.
                    Pretend you are your own
    descendent.
                    Assume he's thinking
    what you're thinking here
    of your progenitors.
                    Presto!
                            The center
    of your world diminishes from you
    the nucleus to you a link
    between begettings—you a fragment
    of a sentence in a chapter of a book
    that never ends.
                    Despite
    the solidarity, you feel like someone
    lost in the Sahara or abandoned
    on the Baltic, miles from shore.
You shrink into a speck among
    so many on so vast a scale.
You melt and shrivel in the way
    old lovers wilt when those
    they love stop loving back,
    love someone else, or love
    unworthily the mere profanity

of things.
            To mock this fate
what good are plaques, engravings
on a stamp, memorials of stone,
remembrances in poetry and song,
or myths perpetuated to the very
stars.
         Your shriveling persists.
You face the fact of disappearance
and the fear thereof.
                  You try
to slow each minute as it flees.
You see why loners might consider
death by choice no longer
a temptation but a right.
                   You learn
that perpetuity and immortality
are differently at last alike
in what they tell you of yourself.
One says your life is history's—
a footnote on a page, if that.
The other says you're God's, and that
means only what it means to God.

LINES AT SEA ON LOVE AND DEATH

1

Remembering the perfect rainbow
   that bridged the port in Domenica
   where a freighter loaded
   with bananas bound for Britain
   blocked my view of a schoolbus
   crushed beneath a giant oak
   toppled by Hurricane David
   and left there as a shrine to death
   by chance, I think of you,
   Judge Jean Follain, pre-occupied
   and by yourself that evening
   on the Place de la Concorde
   when the veering taxi charged
   like a high, blind wind
   with you oblivious and in the way.

2

Watching an inchworm scrunching
   and extending, scrunching and extending
   on a mango leaf in the garden,
   the house-girl from Nevis bunches
   the sheets from the honeymoon suite
   against her bulge so that she looks
   twice-pregnant until the sheet-
   musk and the peeled banana
   left uneaten on the breakfast tray
   remind her of the night she scrunched
   beneath him in the laundry room
   as he inched deeper on his kneecaps
   and repeated she was different, different . . .

3

The ship's wake at midnight
    widened white but flattened
    back to Caribbean ink
    that matched the ace of spades
    the blackjack dealer fingered
    in the bright casino while half
    a mile underneath the keel
    the Santa Teresa de Colón
    with all hands still aboard
    and half a billion in coin
    and bullion barreled in her fo'c'sle
    shifted deeper on a shelf
    of sand that left the barnacled
    mermaid mounted on the white
    unburied prow still pointing
    like a compass straight at Spain.

4

Smelling like the aftersweat of sex,
    the leftover swordfish-sections
    scraped from supper dishes
    into garbage drums and mixed
    with crimson lettuce leafage
    and the grinds of ebony espresso
    waited for the galleymen
    to wheel the drums astern
    and dump the bites and bones
    of what began in water
    in the first place back to brine
    and all the underwater mouths
    that gathered to receive rejections
    from the captain's table while the captain
    and his special guests sipped
    crème de menthe and sucked their cigarettes.

5

After dabbing her armpits dry,
   she lay spreadeagled on her towel
   smoothly squared across the bed
   and memorized her body in the angled
   mirror like a country waiting
   for discovery while, three decks down,
   the purser, knowing that it took
   another's body touching his
   to make him feel his own,
   noticed how a mountain on St. Kitts
   recalled the soft slope
   of his wife's hip and thigh
   when she lay bare beside him
   in her sleep and how her skin
   became a fresh geography he saw
   with either hand whenever
   he touched her for the first
   and only time, again and again.

ARISTOTLE AND THE SNOW

The calendar claims it's spring,
    but January's not convinced.
Last night it froze and browned
    the buds of the magnolia, iced
    the tulip blades, and whitened
    all the yellow hyacinths to prove
    it was asleep, not dead.
                Like tulips
and magnolias, I assumed the zero
months were past.
             I'd changed
my snow-treads, stored
my gloves, and waited for the blooms
that now must wait another
April . . .
        The more I think
of this, the more it widens
into more than weather.
            Isn't
it true that doom seems nearer
just when things are going well?
In Greek they even have a word
for this.
        And wasn't Aristotle
right to say the worst
tragedy is when the worst
happens after we think
the worst is over?
         Perhaps
I'm picking at details, but truth,
like God, hides often in details.
Moravia's *Two Women* proves it . . .
A mother and her daughter hike
    through German lines and reach
    the British zone near Vallecorsa.

Behind them—pillage, hunger,
    bombing, strafing, slaughter.
They celebrate by sleeping in a church
    where suddenly they're raped and left
    for dead by renegade Moroccans.
Ironic?
        Yes.
                Improbable?
                        No.
And just as unexpected as this
    morning's frost that came
    when everything was on the verge
    of blossoming.
                Some people say
I'm droll to think like this.
I'm not.
        I see the same
    absurdity when good things
    happen by surprise.
                The dreams
    of possibility keep hatching
    into facts, for better or for worse.
They don't announce themselves.
They leave us grateful or alone
    and silent with our scars—
    defenseless either way, and wondering.

ALL ELSE BUT SHARING IS A SIDESHOW

Whoever teaches anybody anything is doing
God's work. —A SKI INSTRUCTOR

When you were born, I prayed
    to live until you came of age.
Now that you have, I live
    to see you happy in your work,
    married to someone I can kid
    and spoil, a father yourself.
Forget we're almost forty
    years apart.
              What you admire
I admire: Romeo's last words,
the Brandenburg Concertos, and the pop
a baseball makes when it meets
the sweet spot of a swung bat.
What rankles you still rankles me:
    pontificators, liars, loudmouths,
    and all who start their conversations
    with conclusions.
               Better, we say,
to think and let think.
                Where else
but there and when but then
can anybody grow?
             No wonder
that we work as eldering
students among the younger
ones, learning as much from them
as they from us.
           Remember
the dying girl who told you,
"I love music because I—
I can make it."
          Or the nurse

who wrote me of a husband
who deserted her but whom
she couldn't not love regardless:
"Hope is to love like a bubble
in the stem of a goblet—a defect."
What are such words but gifts
we somehow don't deserve?
                                    Like life
rewarding us with life,
they salvage from the worst of days
whatever says the God of Shakespeare,
Bach, and baseball has a claim
on each of us.
                        Why else
do we accept each given day
as time to try our damnedest
and presume it makes a difference?
That's not what passes for success
these days, or heroism, or the stuff
of sanctity.
                    But it's enough,
and what it gives is everlasting.

Within you there's a "thief
  of fire."
          He wants to crisp
the universe and see it rise
again in words that spark
and smolder on a page.
              That's why
you never start by saying
you will write a poem.
              Poetry
writes you, and all it's after
is perfection in its own good time.
Much of it's work, but most
  of it's luck.
          Whatever it means
may come a-sudden when you see
your shaven whiskers salt
a sink.
         Or while you're watching
toads in tandem breathe
like bladders on a log.
              Or even
as you float asleep into the worst
of midnights.
          Awake, you'll look
more closely at the world
but from a distance.
           Patterns
in your open palm may read
like rivers on a map.
           Willows
in high winds may twist and wail
like ancient widows screaming
at the sky.
         You'll understand

the pilot who could overfly
a battlefield and say, "From the air
even hell looks beautiful."
That's your address . . .
                        The air.

PANACHE

Portraits of Madame du Barry
   and her sister "horizontals"
   show us powdered women
   in chantilly wigs.
                Each bares
one breast.
           Its twin stays hidden
   under taffeta and frills.
As hedonism goes, that's coy.
Forget the caves of Caracalla.
When everything's revealed, what else
   is there to see?
          These lovers
of perfume, of what can be
enhanced, of what provokes—prefer
nudity without nudism.
                Whatever's
beautiful as is they leave
alone.
       Whatever's not, they beautify.
I've seen an iron railing
   spare a tree by circumventing it.
In my United States the tree'd
   be axed.
         I've heard a Frenchman
break the rules of speech to say
a word the way it ought
to sound.
        For love or beauty
every rule's at risk.
             It's French
to sleeve a rose in cellophane.
It's French to make the piquant
   female ass a kind
   of rearward-looking face.

It's French to parsley pork.
It's French to sauce.
                        Confronted
    with unpleasantness, the French
    become unpleasantly correct.
Involved in matters unnegotiable,
    the French will not respond.
                        Questioned,
    they question the questioner or react
    like Killy at Grenoble.
                    When asked
    if winning three Olympic golds
    before de Gaulle himself
    might be the high point of his life,
    he smiled at his skis and answered,
    "In my sporting life."
                    Likewise,
    in *Le dejeuner sur l'herbe* Manet
    permits two men to lunch
    and linger with a naked woman.
One man keeps looking at her total
    face.
        The woman looks at us
    as if to say, "See here, this privacy
    is ours.
            If you must wonder
    why I sit like this among
    these cavaliers, keep wondering.
It's no concern of yours,
    and I do not explain to anyone."
That's frank.
                That's typical.
                        That's French.

THE BODIES OF WOMEN

Some say they just reflect "the nightly
    love of the sea and the moon."
But life and physiology have never
    rhymed.
                Think of the squat
    queen who tranced Mark Antony
    and Caesar with her glances to become
    all Egypt to them both.
                        Or dancers
    who have spines like spears
    and walk as if mere walking
    were a dance.
                Or nurses in their
    white, sure, soft
    shoes, nimble as prancers
    in motion and just as self-possessed.
Such poise and prowess are the stuff
    of mystery.
                And mystery it is.
What else but mystery embues
    a woman of stature to subdue
    a mob with nothing but a stance
    or stare?
             Or tells why men
    or countrymen can languish
    with their goddess gone?
                    Learning
of Piaf's death, Cocteau decided
    not to live.
             For what?
                  For a lifelong
waif whose voice was France
    for half a century.
              And what
of Om Khalsoum who stilled

the Arab world each time she sang
and drew four million (four
million!) to her funeral?
                        Or Marilyn
Monroe whose public grows
and grows?
                Is this bewitchery?
Or is it something that will never
    have a name?
                    Or does it simply
mean that women live within
their bodies to the end—and past
the end?
                Not so for men
who seem to leave their bodies
as they age, regarding what was once
an instrument as now a thing
of no or little use.
                        For those
whose destination is themselves,
what are such losses but a nuisance,
not a destiny?
                    Compared to love
or happiness or children, they appear
at best as vanities.
                        See
for yourselves.
                    The eyes of any
woman say it takes more bravery
to be and bear than to beget.
Or finally just be, with no
    defenses, no illusions, no regrets.

LOSERS KEEPERS

It could be paltry as a pipe,
   a pen, a single sock . . .
Or sacred as a ring, a book
   inscribed by Maritain in French . . .
Or anything made yours by purchase,
   luck, or preference, then lost
   somehow somewhere beyond
   retrieval.
               Suddenly you wake
   to find the customarily misplaced
   transformed into the definitely missing.
Slowly you re-trace your steps.
You make allowance for the inconceivable—
   "No one would leave a wallet
   in a microwave, but still I'll check."
At last you're narrowed to accept
   the obvious while hoping like a jilted
   lover for a totally surprising
   reconciliation in the end.
                        Meanwhile,
   you burn, you damn, you smoulder.
Later you realize you've gained
   through loss all sense of gratitude
   you lost by having.
                  You wonder then
   if everything deserves misplacement
   once to prove how irreplaceable
   it is and how it's always found anew
   in the remembering.
                  All this occurs
   to you one mortal evening
   while you're seeking one lost
   thing made infinitely dearer
   for the losing.
                  A mirror traps you

as you search, and suddenly you're face
to face with someone destined
to be found among the many
waiting, waiting to be lost.

THOSE WHO HAVE GONE BEFORE BUT STAY

The dead are never absent, just invisible.
                                    —YVES MONTAND

The sicknesses have yet to happen
    that will shrink them into patients
    in a future that's already past . . .
My father's frying eggs
    in olive oil.
                        Upstairs,
    my mother's bathing us for bed.
My grandfather and grandmother wage
    backgammon on the kitchen table.
My grandfather's not winning.
For his sake my grandmother's trying
    her best to lose but isn't.
My uncles and their wives have gone:
    Elias and Anna back to Uniontown,
    Aphia and George to Beelermont.
My definite Aunt Katherine,
    the least outgoing but of all
    the most devoted and the most
    courageous, stitches in her room.
Nobody's sick or threatened.
Nobody's died since Frances Mae.
But where's the music in this dream?
I knew and loved these people.
They sang together, joked,
    ate eggs from the same plate.
One by one I hear them laugh,
    then see how quietly they ended,
    one by one.
            ˒   In time
each ending made complete
what seemed so merciless
and unexpected when it happened . . .

But that took years to see.
                          God's
        fugitive is how they've left me—
        a pilgrim spared by luck and facing
        the indefinite—a jigsaw puzzle
        waiting to be solved, except
        the final piece is missing.

TO STOP AND BE STOPPED IN LOURMARIN

Monsieur Camus, you gave
    the stone of our absurdity a name.
Daily we roll it to our graves.
There's no reprieve.
                Regardless,
    you believed we'd never come
    alive until we chose to live
    without appeal for living's
    sake alone.
            Such choices
    put self-murder in its place.
Later, you wrote that we are best
    when we rebel—against the casual
    unfairness of this world, against
    acceptance and the cowardice
    it hides, against rebellion
    itself.
          Rebelling with your pen,
    you called the evil of our age
    our willingness to kill within
    the law.
         You cited war
    and punishments called capital.
Today you'd add the legal
    murders of the undesirable,
    the old, the differently religious,
    or the merely different and the not
    yet born.
         But why go on?
You wrote as poets write.
You showed our shame to us
    and stopped us like a stroke.
For you real justice meant
    how daringly we face the unavoidable
    while struggling for the unattainable.

Because your words defined
    our century the way a hub
    defines a wheel, I've come
    with other pilgrims here to pay
    my last respects.
                    Standing
    beside your name and life-dates
    nicked in rock, I disagree
    with history.
                    Your elegists believed
    your sudden death by accident
    near Villeblevin was premature.
If you could speak, you would
    have said that chance makes
    nothing premature, that lifetimes
    never end the way they should . . .
But what is all this disquisition
    to the life of Lourmarin?
                    The flowers
    of the sun return its Cyclops
    stare the way they always did.
Sweet lavender grows wild
    across your grave.
                    The vineyards
    turn the wind to musk.
                    And all
    the never-to-be-duplicated clouds
    look undisturbed and indestructible.

THE ORDER OF DISORDER

Picasso said he was a messy
    painter.
           Paint splashed the walls,
the floor, the carton of Gitanes
beside the bucket where his brushes
    soaked.
           But look at the results.
Les Demoiselles d'Avignon.
                Guernica.
The lithographs of man as minotaur . . .
And what about Hart Crane?
Locked in his room with all
    that booze and typing paper
    and Ravel's *Bolero* blaring
    like an anthem in his private war,
    he surfaced with *The Broken Tower*
    done . . .
           Each time I frown
and fish for words, I think
of them.
           If writing well
means failing as successfully as possible,
I'd like to fail, if possible,
as nobly as I can.
             If that means
littering my desk, I'll litter.
If that means filling journals
    with fifty versions of one poem,
    I'll fill.
           Somehow it seems
as unpredictable as making love.
Who worries if the phone's ringing
    or the sheets tangled or the garbage
    waiting to be emptied or the shower
    running?

Sometimes some things
are best ignored.
What messes up
our lives might well be life
insisting on its rights or God
asserting His anonymous authority.
They leave such unexpected, irreplaceable,
and sacred gifts but always
time enough to tidy up . . .
This makes me think of how
my father cooked.
On impulse
he'd decide on, say, a stew
he'd make from scratch.
No one
could interfere.
The kitchen turned
into a dump for bean-tips,
meatfat trimmings, onion
shellings, and tomato seeds.
My wife would cringe and shrug
since she'd be stuck with cleaning
up the whole damn mess
when he was through.
My father
mixed and mixed his brew,
regardless.
So what if sauce
speckled his shoe?
So what
if stains were on his favorite
tie, his trousers, and his shirt?
For Dad the gold was always
in the pot.
The rest was dirt.

MATES

Here we are at plus sixty.
Our shared four decades blur
    like landscapes viewed from a train.
Not that we've never paused
    or stopped.
                    Births and funerals
    and marriages made sure of that.
But all the in-betweens
    we almost can remember seem
    in retrospect like trivia beside
    importances . . .
                    Tonight we share
    a living room we've shared
    for half our lives.
                    It's over-
    populated with the lost but no
    less loved.
                    Some nights
    we name them in the present tense,
    forgetting.
                    Or is it not forgetting?
God, how typical we've grown . . .
We sit here wondering how long
    the shortness of our lives will last.
As usual this brings us back
    to what we'll miss the most.
Our son and Dawn, two brothers,
    family, friends, a little loyal
    dog . . .
                    Instead of looking backward
    or ahead, we look around
    and see that everything is movable,
    removable—and momentary
    as this apple that I'm coring.
Shiney with applewax and ripely

hard, it beckons us
to chew it, chew it now,
chew it now before
it yellows.
           And so
you smile, I offer, and we do.

FAILINGS

I've never learned to be
    as private as the French in public.
Not hiding what I feel,
    I fool no one.
             Lately
    I've added to my "faults" by not
    remembering addresses, birthdays,
    and the very names of friends
    I've known for years.
               The present's
    not the past updated to this minute
    anymore.
            So much keeps intervening
    that I live in permanent arrears
    like some disoriented motorist who's lost
    but hopes to make the right
    connection from the wrong direction.
Mostly I fail, but what
    I learn from failing makes me
    glad I failed.
           Why should
    I fret about forgetting the forgettable
    if what I can't forget is all
    that matters?
           Why should I hide
    my private face behind
    a public mask?
           Tell me—
    are we alive to play at living
    or to make a life?
           If living's
    like the tissued, folded, flattened,
    buttoned, pinned, and cellophaned
    perfection of a new dress shirt,
    the joke's on us.

But what
if it's a mystery that dreams us
back to fact the way
that sleeping with a watch on
leaves us handcuffed to the world
no matter what we dream?
Unable to be learned or earned,
the answers never answer
when we ask.
                    They make us wait
as babies wait the backslap
that will sting them into life—as fishers
wait for fishing lines to zip
and zigzag from a strike—as poets
wait for what will overwhelm them
when it comes.
                    It's waiting,
as I'm waiting now, to end
what waiting quietly began.
It's taken all my life . . .

AT THE SITE OF THE MEMORIAL

1

No soldiers choose to die.
It's what they risk by being
    who and where they are.
It's what they dare while saving
    someone else whose life means
    suddenly as much to them
    as theirs.
            Or more.
                    To honor them
    why speak of duty or the will
    of governments?
                    Think first of love
    each time you tell their story.
It gives their sacrifice a name
    and takes from war its glory.

2

Seeing my words in stone
    reminds me of a grave . . .
Not that the words are wrong,
    but seeing them so permanent
    makes me feel posthumous as those
    commemorated here.
                    Lawson,
    Gideon, Butler, Pinder,
    Port, Sarnoski, Shughart . . .
Stephanie Shughart tells me,
    "Randy and I had twenty-two
    months."
                She smiles as if
    to prove that gratitude and grief
    can be compatible.
                    I want

to believe her . . .
                        Brady, who saved
5,000 men by Medivac
and lived, reads every dead
man's name as if it were
his own.
                    He'll read them in his dreams . . .
Next to the next of kin,
    I think how all these men
    risked everything for something
    more than living on.
                        Life meant
    not one more day for them
    but one more act.
                        Just one . . .

SWEET MONEY

I like to purchase things
    with pay I've earned right after
    I've earned it: red delicious
    apples in a chip, steel pliers
    that grip and clamp, a clarinet,
    maduro cigars, T-shirts
    for Sam, milk-chocolate-bark
    with almond chips for Mary Anne.
Don't ask me to explain.
                  No matter
    what I buy, the buying's sweet,
    the price irrelevant.
                My closest
    parallel is how it feels
    to earn the prize of April
    by sticking out the whole winter.
Savers would never understand.
They earn to keep, to keep,
    to keep.
          They're like those rummy
    players who retain their "lays"
    so they can play them jump
    and thump and trump the opposition.
Of course, they run the risk
    of being caught with all
    their "lays" in hand, which smacks
    of dying with your fortune still
    unspent, which Andrew Carnegie
    called the ultimate disgrace . . .
I love to buy before
    I start to gloat on gains,
    before my fingers learn to clutch,
    before I sink and wallow
    in the over-thinking that is death . . .
Last night I visited the truly

dead and saw the coffined
fingers bound with beads.
I thought of hands in handcuffs
  cramped like birds in a trap, useless
  and limp forever.
              That spoke
to me of more than what
it means to buy.
              How should
we live?
          When shall we die?

ONCE UPON A WEDDING

For Sam and Dawn

Watching two lives converge
    through all your predecessors down
    the centuries to you is miracle
    enough.
                But all that is
is history.
                    You're more than that.
If choosing is the most that freedom
    means, you're free.
                    If choosing
    one you love for life
    is freedom at its best,
    you're at your best today.
No wonder we're exuberant.
Today's become an instant
    anniversary for all of us.
You've brought us back to what's
    the most important choice
    of all.
              You've shown that where
    we come from matters less
    than who we are, and who
    we are is what we choose
    to be . . .
             We're all familiar
    with the risks.
               No matter how
    or whom we love, we know
    we're each on loan to one
    another for a time.
              We know
    we're God's employees picked
    for unforeseen assignments

we'll be given on the way.
                         The secret
is to love until the summoning,
regardless of the odds . . .
                         Go now
together in the unison of mates.
Go happily with all our hopes
   and all our blessings.
                         And with God's.

AND THE LOT FELL TO MATTHIAS

For Brendan Galvin

Admit it.
        We're all in training
to become ancestors.
                Accepting that,
we're set to live with memorables:
the furled umbrellas of half-masted
flags—the way French poetry
recited by Laurent Terzieff
becomes whatever electricity is—
the insolence of city streets that slice
through one another at full speed
and keep on going—Jane in profile
with the face of a girl, the smile
of a bride, and a loosely brushed
storm of gray-white hair,
unpinned.
        Confusing as it sounds,
what are we finally but irreplaceably
replaceable replacements, Matthiases,
carriers on?
                Somewhere in our genes
survives a history that leads us
back to then and up to now.
This proves we're mortally immortal.
But why?
        Merely to keep
the chain going?
                To finish
what began with God?
                        To stop
the world and leave it better
even as it wheels?
                Stopping

the world's not difficult.
                                It's all
a matter of pressure, provided
it's precise and timely.
                                One hoof
of Mrs. O'Leary's cow
destroyed Chicago.
                                Truckers,
the traveling hermits of our time,
can be distracted to their deaths
by one persistent hornet in the cab.
And what of Aristophanes, who wakened
    women to the weapon of their loins?
Fed up with burying husbands or sons
    born homeward on their shields,
    the wives of Greece decided
    not to mate until their men
    chose peace.
                                Wars ended in five
days—the average male continence.
When God's prognosticators warn
    of nuclear destruction, plague,
    starvation, or contaminated rain,
    tell them that plumbers could undo us
    in a week by fixing nothing.
                                No,
not a week—a day at most.
But shutting down the world
    stops short of making beautiful
    the merely given.
                                There's the challenge.
Some do it with words.
                                Others
    by touch.
                                A few by martyrdom.

But most by waking daily to their work
    and doing that as conscientiously
    as possible . . .
                Yet first we must reverse,
converse, rehearse the contribution
    only we can give.
             We must denude
ourselves the way we let
    the bodies of our death subside
    in momentary suds.
             Beclothed
in nothing but our skin, we towel
    dry and saunter naked later
    in our clothes until we sleep.
Freudians insist we go
    from tomb-like wombs to womb-like
    tombs.
          I say we go
    from baths to beds by way
    of prologue, traipsing from frothy
    faucetings to replicas of casketry.
Farfetched?
        Not while we watch
    our forked and lathered selves
    asprawl and weightless in a tub.
The toweling can wait.
             The work
can wait.
          The world can wait . . .
That's just the point.
          Entubbed
or abed, we're off our feet.
We're off the world.
         Goodbye
ambition, travel, destinations,

speed, and any time o'clock.
Stockstill, we're primed for anywhere—
    plus everywhere we close our eyes
    to see—plus somewhere only
    Lazarus and Jesus visited
    but spoke of never.
                To all
    the vertical we give their upright
    due.
          For good or ill
    they run the world.
               We choose
    the nude and paganized who languish
    to receive the golden varnish
    of the sun.
             Or children whose domain
    is never higher than the floor.
At least they're closer to the last
    address that's everybody's destination.
Give us for once the laziness
    of prone or supine lovers
    who create with just themselves
    the only time that counts.
Give us Diogenes whose one
    possession was his tub.
               Beside Diogenes,
    who cares if Alexander called himself
    the Great?
          Progenitors and predecessors
matter least.
         Matthias the saint
    succeeded Judas, after all.
              As for philosophy?
Name one philosopher who smiles.
The more we know, the less

we feel.
      And feeling's all
that saves us.
         It hurries us
to make the most of what's
at hand.
        It wants to help,
but first it must be asked.
So stop.
      Stop reading this.
           Ask.

THE HOLY SURPRISE OF RIGHT NOW

*If you can see your path laid out ahead of you
step by step, then you know it's not your path.*
                                    —JOSEPH CAMPBELL

Inside Brooks Brothers' windows
      it's July.
                  Sportshirts on sleek
dummies speak in turquoise,
polo, Bermuda, and golf.
Outside, it's very much the first
      of March.
                  The sportshirts say
today's tomorrow and the present
tense be damned.
                        They tell me
to forget that *here's* the only place
we have.
                  They claim what matters
most is never now but next.
I've heard this argument before.
It leaves me sentenced to the future,
      and that's much worse than being
      sentenced to the past.
                              The past
at least was real just once . . .
                                    What's
called religion offers me the same.
Life's never what I have
      but what's to come.
                              But where
did Christ give heaven its address
except within each one of us?
So, anyone who claims it's not
      within but still ahead is contradicting
      God.

But why go on?
I'm sick of learning to anticipate.
I never want to live a second
    or a season or a heaven in advance
    of when I am and where.
I need the salt and spices
    of uncertainty to know I'm still
    alive.
                It makes me hunger
    for the feast I call today.
It lets desire keep what
    satisfaction ends.
                    Lovers
remember that the way that smoke
remembers fire.
                    Between anticipation
and the aggravation of suspense, I choose
suspense.
                I choose desire.

Index of Titles